Palaeontology

an introduction

James Scott

Palaeontology

an introduction

Illustrations by Sheila Scott

KAHN & AVERILL, LONDON

First published in 1973 by Stanmore Press Ltd
under their associated imprint: Kahn & Averill
Copyright © 1973 James Scott
This book may not be reproduced, in whole or
in part, without permission. Application with
regard to any use of any part of this volume
should be addressed to the publishers.

ISBN 0 900707 22 4

Printed in Great Britain by Willmer Brothers Limited, Birkenhead

Contents

1 Fossils

'Speak to the earth, and it shall teach thee . . .' Job 12:8

Palaeontology is the study of fossils, and fossils are the remains of life from past ages. Even the earliest species of *Homo sapiens* (man) lived long after the disappearance of the dinosaurs and one can in fact 'date' rocks—that is, estimate their age—by studying the fossils contained in them. After tilting (through earth movement) has been allowed for, rocks containing fossil men consistently occur above those preserving the bones of the great dinosaur reptiles and it follows that the latter belong to an earlier age than the human remains.

This last statement introduces one of the basic concepts of palaeontology, which is that rocks of the same age contain the same kind of fossils. If one needs to know the age of a rock quantitatively then the fossils alone are not enough and we have recourse to other methods, such as mineral radioactivity. Fossils are generally used to determine *relative ages* and can be quite exact for this purpose. Relative ages are very useful in mapping; a geologist working away from his home territory can, upon recognizing certain fossils in the exposed rock, determine the age of the rock he is examining. Rocks containing men are Quaternary in age; if they contain dinosaurs they are Mesozoic, and so on.

But problems constantly arise. Certain fossils are more reliable than others in providing age-relationships, or there may be no fossils at all in the rock, or perhaps they are present but can only be identified—and hence compared—by a museum expert. These problems besetting the field geologist are, by utilizing the international information service which has been built up, seldom insoluble. Fossils can also be 'looked up' in reference books, or sent away for expert identification.

Palaeontology is not a dead, dry science, but a tool constantly employed by man to further his understanding of the earth and it may be added that within the earth there are fabulous riches. Oil

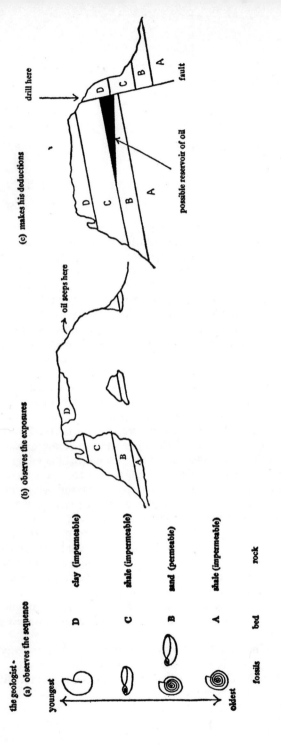

the geologist -

(a) observes the sequence

youngest

D   clay (impermeable)

C   shale (impermeable)

B   sand (permeable)

A   shale (impermeable)

oldest

fossils   bed   rock

(b) observes the exposures

→ oil seeps here

(c) makes his deductions

drill here

fault

possible reservoir of oil

Fig. 1   *Oil-finding*

is found by using a combination of methods among which palaeontology and its modern off-shoot, micropalaeontology, is very important. The presence of oil is established by learning the structure of the rocks in the earth's crust and this structure is determined by knowing the ages of the rocks. This method is illustrated in Fig. 1. In this figure are depicted (a) the sequence of fossils (the oldest being at the bottom) which the geologist would draw up as a preliminary to a closer study of his area, (b) the appearance of the area as it is at the surface, part of it being clearly-visible rock and part mantled over with débris and vegetation, and (c) the geologist's predictions of the underground structure based on his consideration of (a) and (b). The fossil sequence has enabled him to establish the age-relationships of the rocks, and he has seen that beds A, B, C, and D do not continue across the area in an undisturbed fashion as one might at first expect, and that therefore they have been disrupted by earth-movements which would have caused a fault, which in turn would account for the observed oil-seep—the oil escapes through the crushed rock of the fault. Sand, being permeable, would act as a reservoir for the oil, and the inferred fault would prevent large-scale escape for the oil. The details of oil geology need not concern us here, the principle to be illustrated being that the fossils have enabled the underground structure to be clarified.

Also water, iron, coal, gravel, and many other natural resources, would all be far more difficult to obtain but for the information provided by palaeontology. The palaeontologist is not, of course, the only maker of maps: topographical and geophysical maps are of equal importance. Indeed there is an army of teachers, research workers, museum curators and numerous others who contribute to the mass of knowledge on which the geologists rely to make their deductions.

Out of all this work, sometimes apparently even by accident, emerge the clues to the history of life itself, which is the concern of this book.

A FEW TECHNICALITIES

Before plunging into the subject of palaeontology certain terms need defining. These have been kept to a minimum. They have also been not too rigidly defined, for, to have done so would have proved too cumbersome for the general reader, at this stage.

   calcareous: composed of calcium carbonate ($CaCO_3$), which
      occurs in a variety of forms, such as limestone.
   genus and species: the name of a fossil or living organism may

be referred to casually as, e.g. the woolly mammoth, or exactly,
in this case, *Mammuthus primigenius*. *Mammuthus* is the name
of the genus, and is a group of organisms of which one sub-
group is *Mammuthus primigenius*, which is the name of the
species. Several species may therefore be expected to make up
one genus. *Homo sapiens* is the name of our species: the rival
species belonging to the genus *Homo* seem to have died out
long ago in the struggle for survival. (Note the use of capital
and small letters.)

kingdom, phylum, class, order: these are units used in classification. Kingdom is the largest—in our own case Animalia
(animals), of which a subdivision is the Phylum Chordata
(animals with a spinal cord), then Class Mammalia (mammals),
then Order Primates (apes, monkeys, man, etc.). Finally, one
comes down to genus and species.

geological column: the history of the earth, or part of it, represented diagrammatically. Fig. 2 illustrates this.

nekton: swimming aquatic creatures (fish, whales, squids).

plankton: floating and drifting aquatic creatures (jellyfish, algae).

benthos: creatures living in or on the sea-floor (crabs, clams).

aerial: creatures living normally in the air.

terrestrial: creatures living normally in or on the land.

algae: seaweeds and other lowly plants, often unicellular.

This summarizes some useful terms, and though there are reser-
vations (e.g. some swimmers are too small to keep up with the
currents, and so drift with the plankton), they will do for now.

THE NATURE OF FOSSILS

It is a memorable occasion for anyone when he finds his first
fossil. The excitement may be a little dimmed when he is told that
the fossil is 'just a replacement',* but replaced shells are perfectly
valid, as indeed are the mere footprints and impressions of ancient
creatures' bodies. Most fossils are the shells of lowly sea-creatures
rather than the bones and skulls of great vertebrates. Nevertheless,
many fossils are composed of the original material which belonged
to the animal when it was alive, and vertebrate bones are by no
means rare. A few weeks of practical field-work, aided preferably
by a guide-book of the locality or someone experienced, will pro-

* i.e. the form of the shell is retained although chemical activity
within the rock has dissolved away the original substance of the
shell and replaced it with new material.

duce a great variety of material in most areas. Furthermore, there is no partiality in the fossils for whomsoever they reveal themselves to: a beginner can make a 'find' as readily as an expert, provided he knows where to look.

Fossilization falls into four main categories: the original material, alteration of the original material, impregnation, and the impression of an organism (or its hard parts) on the rock.

(1) Fossilization of original material.

Perfectly preserved organisms are rare. One example is the existence in Siberia of frozen mammoths, extinct species of elephant-like creatures refrigerated, apparently for ever, in the ice. The scavengings of dogs and wolves revealed these fossils to the world, and not only was the hair and flesh still intact, but in some cases even grass lay half-digested between the teeth of the mammoths.

Rather more commonly, original material is found in the form of shells and skeletons of creatures which have been preserved in rock and, except for the lack of flesh, are more or less unaltered. Such fossils may belong to any age, though they are more usually of the later geological periods. This presents one of the main requirements for fossilization, namely the presence of hard parts. Thus a horse, having died, say, in a temperate forest in England, is reduced to a skeleton by pecking crows, gnawing dogs, worms, beetles and other carrion-feeders (there are no vultures in England). The skeleton, already pulled apart by these animals, will eventually be reduced to dust by erosion. Such is the fate of most dead organisms on land. But had the horse stumbled into a bog, or been overwhelmed by blown-dust, or (to extend the example) had we been considering a sea-creature which might have been covered with sand, silt or trapped under a layer of sediment then, though the soft parts would still have eroded away, the hard parts would have been buried and thus become fossils. The lesson of this is that only *some* of the life existing at any particular time is likely to provide fossils, and even then one is not necessarily going to find a representative selection of the life prevalent at the time in question. Thus, in the case of the horse, its stumbling into a bog would have been no guarantee that any other horses would also have stumbled into the bog. This imbalance of the fossil evidence of the life of the past, coupled with the destructive effects of the passage of time, is reflected in Professor Ager's remark that palaeontologists studying the ecology of ancient life are not dealing with 'the living inhabitants of the village, but only the bodies in

the churchyard, and then only after many visits by grave robbers'.
(2) Alteration of original material.
This is probably the most common type of fossilization. Once the
hard parts are buried and have become part of the earth's crust,
they generally become affected, sooner or later, by the ever-present
water which soaks down through the joints and crevices in the rock,
dissolving mineral salts as it seeps. This water will come into contact with the fossil shell and cause the material of the shell to
recrystallize, or to be replaced by new minerals hitherto held in
solution by the water. In this fashion an ordinary shell of calcium
carbonate may be replaced by, say, iron sulphide, either as iron
pyrites (which is stable to the atmosphere), or marcasite (which is
not). Both these forms of iron sulphide have a beautiful brassy
appearance much prized by fossil collectors, but unfortunately the
marcasite fossils will turn to dust unless treated and lacquered soon
after being dug out of the rock.
Alteration may not necessarily imply replacement: thus the
breakdown of wood to form coal does not necessarily involve
extraneous material.
(3) Impregnation.
The hard parts of an organism may be preserved, sometimes in
meticulous detail, if the water soaking it as it dies, or percolating
through the rocks after it has been buried, can impregnate it and
introduce minerals which will fill the pores and solidify therein.
As one might expect, only porous materials are prone to this type
of fossilization—wood and sponges are two examples. Wood impregnated by opal occurs as petrified forests: some of the trees still
remain upright in their place of growth.
(4) Impressions and other indirect evidence.
If the rock encasing a fossil is particularly porous, a shell is
likely to dissolve altogether in the percolating water. This leaves
a cavity where the shell was, but the rock may still bear an impression of the outside of the shell on the outside of the cavity, or of
the inside of the shell on the inside of the cavity. Thus one may
find moulds and casts which, though only impressions of shells, are
still fossils in a sense and may convey almost as much information
as 'true' fossils.
One may quote further examples of fossilization. Footprints of
animals in mudstone have been found, evidently preserved before
the next rainstorm could wash them away. Footprints found in the
U.S.A. indicate that a dinosaur walked across some mud in a shower
of rain, sat down, and walked on again a little later. Burrows of
land and aquatic creatures may be found as indirect evidence of

life. The 'Devil's Corkscrews' of North America, which so puzzled the early workers of this area, have since been identified as the hardened infillings of rodents' spiral burrows, exhumed from the softer surrounding soil by erosion. Even more indirect evidence includes the coiled excreta thrown out of the bodies of sea-creatures, the stomach stones of reptiles (these stones were used to grind up tough food, after the fashion of a bird's gizzard), the ropes of sand laid down on the shoreline by burowing worms, and so on.

SOME REMARKABLE EXAMPLES OF FOSSILIZATION

Although it is true that rapid burial and the presence of hard parts are requirements for fossilization, there are exceptions to this rule. Worms and jellyfish exist in the fossil record, preserved under favourable circumstances, and at Wakulla Springs Cave, Florida, mastodon bones occur loose on the cave floor (below 80 ft of water). But in general the rule holds true.

Many are familiar with the golden colour of amber, a light mineral which owes its origin to resin oozing from trees and hardening into lumps which become fossilized. Amber is commonly found on the shores of the Baltic, and in Lithuania there is an amber museum. Much prized by prehistoric man as a gem, it has been found in certain graves of Mycenean Greece (2nd millenium B.C.). More remarkable in palaeontologists' eyes, perhaps, is the occurrence of insects preserved in all their detail, even to the microscopic hairs on their bodies, within the amber, evidently trapped in the resin and gently embalmed.

It is seldom that the skin of an animal is preserved as well as its bones, but the hide of a female woolly rhinoceros from the Pleistocene period has been found in Starunia, Ukraine, preserved by natural oil and salt, the skin even showing scars of wounds sustained in fights. The inhabitants of Salzkammergut, Austria, in the 18th century reported finding the body of a man in one of the salt mines; he was dressed in clothes which no one could recognize. He may well have been an Iron Age man (last few centuries B.C.), who had died in the mines and been preserved by the salt. An even better example of preservation can be seen in the museum at Copenhagen. Here the Danes have on exhibition a man who was buried in a Danish peat bog about the time of Christ, and been perfectly mummified by the acid water of the peat, without, however, the ungainly drying and stretching of the skin which occurs in the Egyptian mummies. This Dane is, in fact, tanned by the peat, like leather. The face of Tollund man, thoughtful and utterly human, is a startlingly vivid object to behold.

EARLY MISTAKES BY PALAEONTOLOGISTS

In the early days of palaeontology a fossil often stood a better chance of being described accurately by the artist than by the palaeontologist. Certain fossil bones were once described as 'Homo Diluvii Testis'—man, witness of (Noah's) flood. The creature may possibly have witnessed a flood, but it is now obvious that it was no man. The bones represented an amphibian—a salamander, in fact. The science soon progressed beyond this uncritical stage, and by the beginning of the 19th century fossils were being described with reasonable accuracy. It remains a curious fact, however, that such was the grip of the Church's dogma on the mind of man, that it was some time before general agreement could be reached to the fact that fossils were the remains of life millions of years old and not 'devices of the Devil' introduced by the Creator to baffle man. The Bible, accepted literally, has been read to date Creation at about 4,000 B.C. Geologists, however, determined the beginning of life to be at least 500,000,000 B.C. and, giving support to inflammatory theories like those of evolution, claimed the descent of man from members of the ape-group rather than from Adam. Of course palaeontologists are no more free from error than other human beings. For instance, graptolites are so named from their resemblance to writing on the rock (Greek: graptos, written + lithos, a stone). Indeed, for many early workers these fossils were inorganic markings—natural graffiti, as it were. Such natural graffiti are known in the igneous rocks. Graphic granite owes its markings to the systematic intergrowth of different types of crystals. But as far as the graptolites are concerned it is nowadays accepted that they are the skeletons of tiny colonial marine organisms, now extinct.

Perhaps the most famous and tragi-comic story of error in palaeontology conerns Herr Johann Beringer, a Professor of Medicine at Würzburg, Germany, in the early 18th century. This worthy had the misfortune to publish descriptions of certain stones carved as a hoax and scattered on the hillsides by his young collectors, Beringer treated them as bona fide fossils. When their true nature was revealed he had to spend much time buying back his own publication in an effort to save face. Few lecturers in palaeontology are free from such students' pranks, though they seldom, it is hoped, reach the publication stage. Almost as renowned as Beringer's

academic débâcle is the Piltdown forgery, a cunning union of a
man's skull and an ape's jaw which deceived experts for years.
(Further description of this occurs in the last chapter.)

FOSSIL NAMES

It might be opportune to mention here a few of the more noteworthy items from the nomenclature of the subject. There is a
fair crop of fossil names which defy pronunciation, like *Bdellacoma*,
Quenstedtoceras, *Tschernyschewia*, and *Stoliczkaia* (though presumably those of central and eastern European origin may disagree with
me here), while other fossils possess laudably descriptive names
(*Titanites giganteus*) or are named from their place of origin
(*Hongkongites*). Some of the older names are melodious and
evocative—*Venus, Chione, Astarte, Leda*—but unfortunately it is
rarely possible to continue this euphony with the flood of new
names. Ideally, a fossil name should say something useful about the
fossil it relates to; thus *Conomitra parva* is conical, mitre-shaped,
and small. Latin and Greek are useful languages for this purpose
in that they are both still widely understood, in a rudimentary form
at least, and bear no national imprint.

DISTRIBUTION OF FOSSILS

Fossils occur in most sedimentary rocks and other than the very
oldest. These latter are called Precambrian and can be regarded,
with few exceptions, as totally devoid of fossils. Of the remaining
rocks, the sedimentary rocks (i.e. those laid down on land or under
water by natural processes such as currents, tides, wind and so on)
generally contain fossils to some extent, though this is by no means
always so. If the rock becomes chemically altered by heat and/or
pressure, a process called metamorphism takes place. The rock
hardens, re-crystallizes, and the fossils within it are destroyed. The
hardest fossils may survive a moderate amount of metamorphism,
though often showing extreme distortion which indicates the great
pressure the rock has been subjected to. Igneous rocks, which usually
started as molten magma, are naturally not the most likely source
of fossils. Yet even in these, shells can be preserved by volcanic
ash falling out of the sky and settling under water as an igneous
type of sediment.

Geographically, fossils are surprisingly widespread. One of the
reasons for Scott's expedition to the South Pole in 1911–12 was the
geological investigation of the interior of Antarctica. His men found

fossil wood, evidence that Antarctica was once a land with a rich cover of vegetation.

There are rocks in Arctic Canada, now the haunt of the polar bear, which contain salts which have apparently crystallized from enclosed bodies of water, under conditions of heat and drought. Some of the highest peaks in the Alps and Himalayas are built of rocks which contain marine fossils. These tell us that the sediment was laid down under the sea. In fact all the evidence of fossils unites in telling us that the nature of the world is not uniform, that its climate has changed, and that the mountains are impermanent.

2 Evolution and Environment

*'I have called this principle, by which each slight variation,
if useful, is preserved, by the term Natural Selection.' – Charles
Darwin – Origin of Species, Ch. 3*

The theory of evolution concerns itself with Neontology (the
biology of living organisms) and Palaeontology. I shall concentrate
on the latter, with a few preliminary remarks of general significance.

THE NATURE OF EVOLUTION

The basic concept of evolution is as follows:
(a) variations in the structure and general appearance of organisms
    are observed to occur;
(b) some of these variations, which may have arisen spontaneously,
    became hereditary, and are thus perpetuated in succeeding
    generations;
(c) though most of these variations may be deleterious, some are
    beneficial;
(d) evolution presupposes the survival of the fittest. Any group of
    organisms, isolated geographically or otherwise and exhibiting
    beneficial variations, will have the advantage over other less
    favoured groups of the same organisms, and the former will
    tend to breed and survive more successfully than the latter.
(e) The consequence of (d) is the evolution of a fitter breeding stock
    which is presumably better adapted to its environment than its
    forbears, and thus a new, hardier species may arise.
One may ask why, if (e) is true, do major groups of plants or
animals ever become extinct? A number of reasons can be given
for extinction, the most common being that the environment
changes faster than the evolution towards a fitter breeding stock.
(By environment we mean not only the inorganic environment;
temperature, salinity, humidity, but also the organic environment;
competitors, predators, parasites, and prey). Having this number
of variables to cope with, it is not surprising that extinctions do

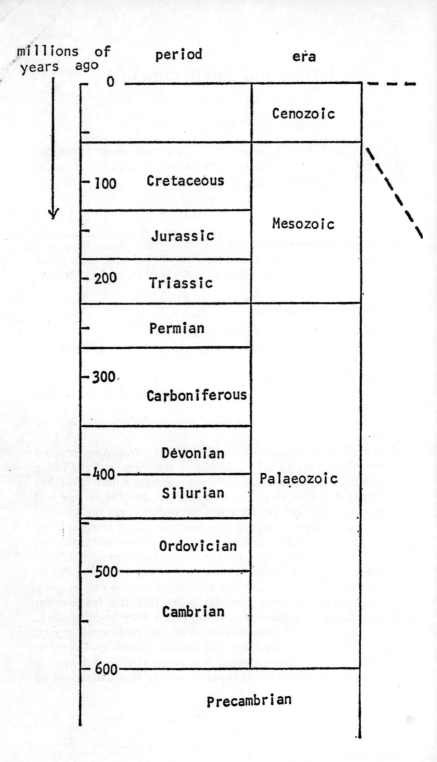

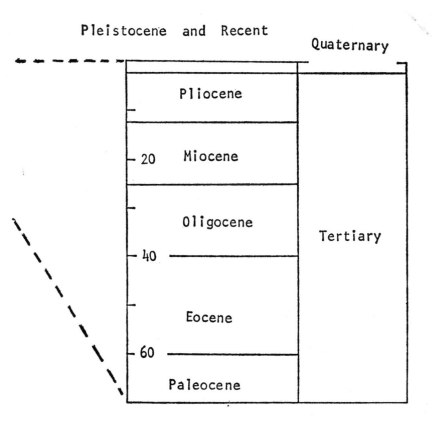

Fig. 2 *The Geological Column*

occur, though the adaptability of the living world is such that extinctions are rare in the larger groups of organisms. Indeed nearly all the major groups of animals have survived since their first appearance in the oldest fossiliferous rocks (Cambrian, see Fig. 2), though, of course, the fate of the minor groups within these major ones has varied considerably throughout geological history.

THE EVOLUTION OF THE HORSE

An excellent palaeontological example of evolution is provided by the fossil history of the horse. The horse itself is something of a palaeontological curiosity; it is one of the few survivors (the rhinoceros is another) of a formerly more diversified order of mammals called the Perissodactyla. The horse runs on a hoof which is built onto the middle toe, in contrast to the Artiodactyla (cow, antelope, buffalo, deer) which mostly run on a cloven hoof which is based on the 3rd and 4th toes. The horse originated as a small, dog-like browser on forest leaves, and later became the tall grazing creature of the plains which we know today. Though its fossils are commonly found in the New World, where the evolution apparently occurred, horses eventually disappeared from there only to re-appear when European man brought it back from its new home in the Old World.

Fig. 3 shows the evolution of the horse and its foot. Notice how the middle toe has grown at the expense of the others, resulting from the abandonment of the pad and the modification to the hoof; an adaptation for running on the hard plains. Another but less obvious change is the modification of the tooth. Early members of the horse family had a low-crowned tooth suitable for browsing on forest vegetation, but in the transition from forest to plains (with concomitant adaptation to a running habit) a solution had to be found to the problem of grit. Grass contains grit which wears down the grass-eater's teeth. But grass, being the obvious source of nourishment on the plains, was an unsuitable diet for low-crowned teeth. Accordingly, a high-crowned tooth evolved, which would not be worn out by constant grass-eating.

THE CONCEPTS OF HOMOLOGY AND HOMOEOMORPHY

The concept of homology does not require any theory of evolution to motivate it, and indeed homology was well-known some time before Darwin and Wallace. But homology, which is best understood with at least some reference to evolution, is the condition where two or more organisms possess organs which may look different at first glance, but have a basic structural similarity which betrays a common origin (or, if one is to omit evolutionary considerations, relate to a common type). Thus the man's hand, the bat's wing, and the seal's flipper are all homologues, and exhibit the phenomenon of homology. If one wishes to prove this, a study of the bones is required (see Fig. 4). Clearly, the bones of a man's

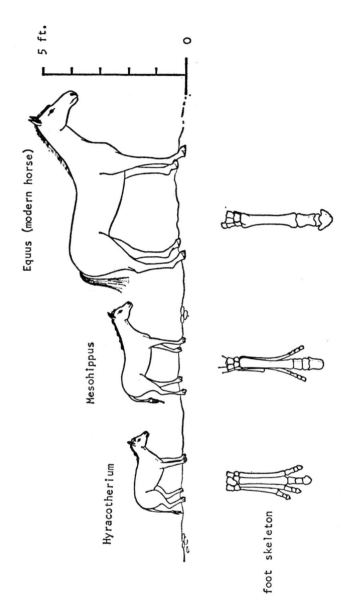

Fig. 3   *The Evolution of the Horse*
(evolution being from left to right in this figure)

hand, bat's wing, and seal's flipper are all of a similar type, and
one could indeed draw from them an 'average' and call it the
'archetype'. It is more profitable, however, to consider the fossil
evidence behind these modern skeletons, and this evidence, though
lamentably discontinuous in parts, suggests strongly that all three
types of appendage, and indeed all mammalian limb-terminating
appendages, are derived from the primitive mammal's hand. This
seems to have been quite similar to our own hand, and indeed one
may say that man's hand is essentially a primitive organ, and that
its marvellous capacity for crafts and skills do not depend on any
pronounced modification of this original organ, but rather on a
lack of it.

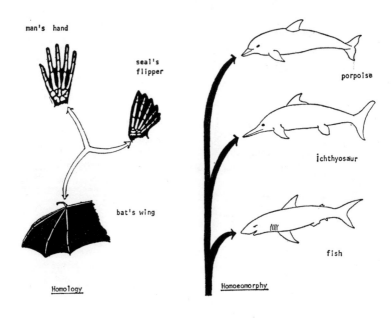

Fig. 4   *Homoeomorphy and Homology*

Homoeomorphy is a condition where two or more organisms look similar, or have parts which look similar but have different origins, or relate to dissimilar archetypes. Thus the whale, the fish, and the ichthyosaur all look similar—they all, as a rule, are streamlined, have two eyes and fin-shape appendages—as shown in Fig. 4. But they are homoeomorphous because their internal structures are different from each other, this being due to the fact that the whale is descended from the primitive land-mammals, the ichthyosaur from the primitive land-reptiles, and the fish from primitive aquatic fish. Of course, homoeomorphy is a purely relative concept: all land vertebrates are descended from fish, and indeed it is a defensible hypothesis that all life is descended from a single origin. But homoemorphy usually relates to more immediate ancestries than that. Although of great interest, homoeomorphy is a nuisance to palaeontologists since it means that many fossils which are grouped together under one name prove, on closer inspection, to belong to several unrelated types and therefore merit the application of more than one name.

IMPERFECTIONS IN THE FOSSIL RECORD

The reason for much of the confusion that exists over fossil names is that only the hard parts of an organism fossilize, and not the soft parts. Rabbits and rodents are homoeomorphous in that they have similar chisel teeth, but a study of these creatures reveals that one is dealing with two totally different mammalian orders, named Lagomorpha and Rodentia respectively. Vertebrate skeletons are sufficiently elaborate in their structure for these two orders to be differentiated, but how is one to deal with simple sea-shells, where, beyond the general shape of the shell there is little to distinguish one shell from the next? Homoeomorphy is, indeed, widespread in the fossil bivalve literature, and though a sequence of evolutionary stages will help to unravel the homoeomorphy of some of the shells, there are many simple fossils of uncertain history which are, in this respect, frankly baffling.

The imperfections in the fossil record take another form. It can be well understood from the general tendencies of the scavenging creatures of the world—wolves, vultures, hyaenas, ants, worms, and their aquatic counterparts—that little in the way of edible flesh or vegetable matter survives for long after its owner's death. Bones are gnawed and crumbled, wood rots, shells disintegrate, and, on the whole, nothing fossilizes unless fairly rapid burial occurs so as to protect the organism's hard parts from decay. As if this were not enough, one has to allow for the fact that many fossils are lost in solution by the water constantly leaking through the earth's crust: others are heated and transformed to metamorphic rock by the earth's heat, and lose their organic identity. The rocks may be eroded away by the rivers or the sea.

In addition to these considerations, one must remember that only a small fraction of the world's fossiliferous rock meets the geologist's hammer. Most of those which are not submerged by the sea are inaccessible by their depth below the earth's surface. Geologists see only a small percentage of even the best-exposed rocks. The fossil record, then, is patchy and discontinuous, and it can be a matter of no surprise that there are so many unanswered questions in palaeontology. Yet it remains true that there is a remarkable amount of information already available from the fossiliferous rocks of the world, and the evolutionary story provided by the fossils is fairly detailed. To illustrate this last remark, consider the evolution of the mammals from the reptiles.

THE MAMMAL-TO-REPTILE EVOLUTION

It is, at the present day, fairly easy to distinguish a mammal from a reptile. Mammals usually have hair, a fairly uniform warm blood-temperature, give birth to live young which they suckle with milk. Reptiles are usually naked or scaly, the blood-temperature depends on environmental conditions, they lay eggs, and do not suckle their young.

But in order to be useful to palaeontologists, such criteria must be extended to refer to bone structure. The mammals have a simple lower jaw-bone (that is, the lower jaw consists of two parts joined at the front), a single opening in the skull for the nose, a set of three ear-bones—malleus, incus, and stapes (hammer, anvil and stirrup)—two sets of teeth during life, and two or more roots to each cheek-tooth. Also, a differentiation of the teeth-row is common (incisors, canine, premolars and molars in the case of man), and there is a secondary palate (the layer of bone at the top of our mouth which separates the mouth from the nasal cavity). These and other skeletal characteristics of the mammals serve to distinguish mammal fossils from reptile fossils, and each has its purpose: thus, the secondary palate is a device to allow the mammal to breathe while it is eating. The reptile, whose nose opens directly into the mouth-cavity, can only breathe between gulps of food, while the single lower jaw-unit of the mammals may be to strengthen it for chewing. Fig. 5 shows how the number of bone-

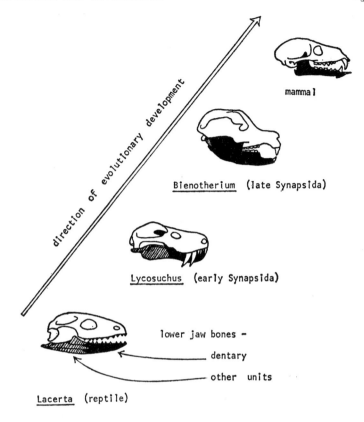

mammal

Bienotherium (late Synapsida)

Lycosuchus (early Synapsida)

lower jaw bones —

dentary

other units

Lacerta (reptile)

direction of evolutionary development

Fig. 5   *The Evolution of the Mammalian Jaw*
(not to scale)

units in each side of the lower jaw has dwindled to one during the evolution from reptile to mammal.

For most mammalian and reptilian fossils, all this is clear enough, but when one turns to deal with the reptilian group, Synapsida, complications arise. The closer one examines these Synapsida the more it appears like Lewis Carroll's Caucus-Race. In a sense, the group as a whole got off to a premature start in that its maximum development was in the Permian and Triassic periods. In succeeding Jurassic and Cretaceous periods, instead of the Synapsida's descendants, the mammals, becoming the dominant land-vertebrates, the reptiles proliferated and the dinosaurs became supreme, with the synapsid-mammal evolution going on in the background, as it were, with the resultant mammals scurrying about as small, unobtrusive creatures. Had the Synapsida been less unfortunate, perhaps the history of life would have been quite different. The air might have been inhabited by bats (which are mammals) rather than birds (which are directly descended from reptiles), and man might have arisen and died out long ago already.

However, this is mere speculation. The facts of the synapsid fossil record show an early tendency to a differentiation of the teeth. *Dimetrodon*, apart from possessing a 'sail' (presumably of skin), supported by spines (of very questionable purpose), had its teeth differeniated into 'incisors', 'canines' and 'molars', in the upper jaw at least. Later synapsids developed a secondary palate, and a lower jaw-bone in which one unit is very large (ultimately to become the single-unit mammalian jaw-bone), the other units being correspondingly small. They also had a more elegant gait with fore-and-aft limb structure, as opposed to the more sprawling elbows-outwards posture of other reptiles.

The implication of the Synapsida story is that one cannot decide exactly where the reptiles end and the mammals begin. The big changeover seems to be a series of uncertain steps rather than a bold, decisive stride. Mammal-like structural characteristics arise independently in more than one group within the Synapsida. Were the creatures later members of the Synapsida, advanced reptiles or primitive mammals? It is hard to say. Probably the possession of warm blood is the clearest indication of mammalhood (apart, of course, from the possession of mammary glands), since this is the key to the nimble way of life which is so characteristic of the mammal class, and it may be identifiable in the presence of the secondary palate, since, whereas a cold-blooded animal can cease breathing during the time it gulps its food, this is very difficult for a warm-blooded creature with its high oxygen requirements. But the secondary palate is already well developed in certain synapsid types which otherwise retain several reptilian characteristics.

In the Ictidosauria—group of fossils provisionally assigned to the later Synapsida—a reptile/mammal transition is indicative of creatures in whose skeletons the only attribute relating them to the reptiles is that the reduction of the number of lower jaw-bones to one (on each side) is not quite complete. One more step, one might say, and the mammals are with us, and, appropriately, definite mammals begin to appear thereafter in the Jurassic period.

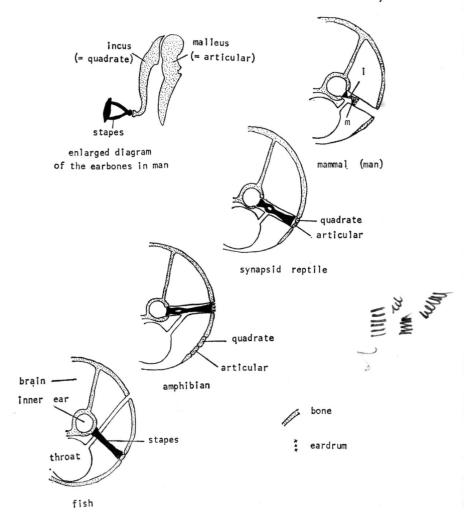

Fig. 6   *The Evolution of the Ear*

THE EVOLUTION OF THE EAR

The ear was originally an organ of balance, a function which it still retains, but with modifications to enable it to pick up vibrations in the ear originating from the outside world—that is, to hear. In the fish, balance is achieved by the action of stones (otoliths) in the fluid-filled chambers: an off-balance fish feels the stone move over the sensitive interior of the ear-chamber, and its brain registers the imbalance, which can then be corrected. As Fig. 6 illustrates, there is also in the fish's ear a special bone (the hyomandibular), which connects the inner ear with the skull, and serves to transmit vibrations in the water (and hence in the skull) to the inner ear. In amphibians, a proper ear-drum is developed, since the vibrations in the air need a more sensitive receiving device than the skull bones. In the Synapsida (reptiles), the same arrangement persists, but two small bones, released from service by the above-mentioned reduction of the number of jaw-bone units are located next to where the ear-drum no doubt lay, and presumably aided sound-transmission. The most remarkable development is to be seen in man, however: the stapes (stirrup), which is homologous with the fish hyomandibular, still operates the inner ear, but it is connected with the ear-drum by the incus (anvil) and malleus (hammer), which are homologous with the two supernumerary amphibian jaw-bone units. Our ear is vastly more complicated than the fish's, of course, but evolutionary studies show that the vital, tiny bones of the middle ear are no more than glorified jaw-bone units of previous eras.

'MISSING LINKS' AND 'LIVING FOSSILS'

Palaeontology is at its most important in matters of evolution when it is dealing with creatures which are now extinct, or supposedly extinct. This reservation is prompted by our experience of the coelocanth (see Fig. 23), a fish belonging to a group (Crossopterygii) which was believed to have died out with the dinosaurs in the Cretateous, and yet found alive in 1938. The main interest of this discovery of a living crossopterygian fish lies in its bone structure. The crossopterygians have been nicknamed 'lobe-fins' with reference to the fleshy lobes at the base of their fins: these lobes contain within them the bone structure which foreshadows the amphibians' leg, ankle, and toes, and hence the leg, ankle, and toes of all other land and aerial vertebrates. Indeed, it would appear that it was a sub-group of the crossopterygians which struggled on to dry-land in the late-Devonian/early-Carboniferous times and began to breathe air and so become amphibians. The other fish (mostly Actinopterygii) declined to leave the water, apart from a few temporary air-breathers, like the mud-skipper of today.

Evolutionary palaeontology is rarely cut-and-dried, and although it is often possible to draw up convincing details of the evolution of a small number of fossils, it is seldom possible to put together these individual steps so as to synthesise a continuous progression through a long succession of changes. Sooner or later a gap appears in the succession: perhaps the relevant fossils have not been found, or they have been found and are not complete, or the evolution was so fast at that particular time that the fossils do not show it in all its stages. This problem is particularly vexatious when one is dealing with the origins of major groups, such as the fish. Occasionally, however, lucky finds of 'missing links' serve to complete an otherwise discontinuous progression, and one such fortunate discovery is that of the Jurassic bird-reptile, *Archaeopteryx*, only two skeletons of which are known. In the table below, the characteristics of *Archaeopteryx* are compared with those of the reptiles and birds:

REPTILES	ARCHAEOPTERYX	BIRDS
1) Long tail skeleton of separate vertebrae as a rule	Long tail skeleton of separate vertebrae	Short tail skeleton
2) Solid bones as a rule	Solid bones	Hollow bones
3) Front limbs resemble rear limbs	Front limbs somewhat similar to rear limbs, and of same length	Wings are modified arms: markedly different from rear limbs
4) Braincase small	Braincase large	Braincase large
5) Teeth usually present	Teeth present	No teeth
6) No feathers	Feathers present	Feathers present
7) Relatively weak support for chest muscles	Weak support for chest muscles	Strong support for chest muscles (to maintain flight activity)

It can be seen that by criteria 1, 2, 5, and 7 these fossils resemble the reptiles, but by criteria 4 and 6 (considered here to be the more important) they are birds. By criterion 3 they are transitional. *Archaeopteryx* (Fig. 7) must have been a rather weak flyer, perhaps preferring to glide (like *Pterodactylus* and other true flying reptiles) rather than fly as birds do today. The structure of the feet suggests that *Archaeopteryx* could perch, and indeed it is to be expected that arboreal surroundings, with all its demands for agility and lightness, would be a precursor to the aerial habitat. These fossils, then, are midway between the reptiles and the birds.

Fig. 7   *Archaeopteryx*

THE PROCESS OF DEDUCING THE PAST ENVIRONMENT FROM FOSSILS

It would be very helpful to the palaeontologist if he could rely on any group of animals or plants to be a trustworthy guide to climatic and other environmental conditions of the past. Unfortunately, this is rarely possible. If, for instance, a future palaeontologist were to describe all tigers as being inhabitants of tropical jungles, he would have to explain the existence of the largest of all, the Manchurian tiger, in the very untropical conditions of south-eastern Siberia. Indeed, the Manchurian tiger has been reported to live as far north as Irkutsk (53° N).

Describing the king-crab group (Limulina) or our sea-shores as 'shallow-water marine' does not help much when we consider its history; in Devonian times the Limulina were mostly marine, in Carboniferous times they were mostly fresh-water. In the Mesozoic Era they were largely fresh-water, but some had also come to favour the brackish water of estuaries. Now they are marine again. On the other hand, some groups do provide firm information; thus, as far as is known, none of the cephalopod molluscs (octopus, squid, etc.) can tolerate fresh-water. The presence of cephalopod fossils is, then, a reliable indication of marine conditions. Out of this tangle of reliable and unreliable data the palaeontologist gropes towards a reconstruction of the past, a task which is fortunately often made easier by non-fossil data. Thus, rain-prints or sun-cracks may be preserved in a bed of clay, giving a hint of the climate of that time. Crystals of salts which formed in evaporating salt lakes suggest an arid or semi-arid climate. Ash of igneous material laid down with the fossils indicates the proximity of volcanoes.

OXYGEN ISOTOPES

Knowledge as to the temperatures of ancient seas can be obtained by estimating the proportions of oxygen isotopes bound up in fossil material. Of the two main isotopes of oxygen present in the air (and hence dissolved in the seas and lakes), O^{16} is the commoner; O^{18} has $\frac{1}{500}$ of the abundance of O^{16}. Since the relative concentrations of the carbonate ions present in sea water containing the various isotopes of oxygen varies according to temperature, and since these carbonate ions can be found in fossil shells as $CaCO_3$, it follows that identification of the oxygen isotopes in the fossil's $CaCO_3$, and accurate measurement of their concentrations, will enable us to determine the temperature of the water in which the shell was formed.

Oxygen-temperature-analysis is based on the above reasoning, though, of course, for the sake of simplicity, I have ignored some of the difficulties. For instance, re-crystallization of the fossil shell. a commonplace phenomenon, will upset the results since the oxygen-isotope-ratio of water percolating through the earth's crust may bear no relation to the isotope ratio of the sea in which the creature originally built its shell. However, with due regard for these factors, some very interesting deductions have been made. Thus, the study of a certain belemnite from the British Jurassic rocks indicates that the average temperature of the Jurassic sea at the time and place at which the creature providing this fossil belonged, was about 18° C. (The seas round Britain average 8–12° C today.)

Belemnites are fossils commonly found in Mesozoic rocks which belonged to marine, tentacle-bearing swimming creatures—the 'belemnoids'—which are now extinct. The living creature looked like the squids and indeed was closely related to them in evolution (Class Cephalopoda, of the Phylum Mollusca). The belemnite (Fig. 8) is the solid bullet-shaped part of the skeleton which, when broken in two, reveals a radial and concentric structure very similar to the rays and rings in a log of wood. The radial structure is due to the radial growth of the calcite crystals: the concentric structure is, like the rings in a tree, presumably due to seasonal growth. The information carried by the oxygen isotopes in the calcite of these concentric rings shows that, as far as the British Jurassic belemnite is concerned (and assuming the species did not undertake large-scale migrations), a seasonal variation of 6° C is indicated, and the belemnite-creature lived at least 3–4 years.

Fig. 8   *Longitudinal section of a Belemnite*

PLANTS

Another source of information is fossil plants. Present-day plants show, on the whole, a clear relationship with their environment, certainly at a cursory glance. Travelling from the poles to the equator one crosses first cold desert, then coniferous forest, then temperate forest, after that perhaps a zone of hot desert, and finally tropical forest. Provided one is dealing with fairly recent fossils whose species are still alive and can be studied today, one can make many useful deductions about the environmental conditions of fossil plants. Older fossils are more difficult to study, but certain facts can be established. Thus, in the classic study of the London

Clay flora (Eocene) of England, it was found that, of the genera of plants in the London Clay, 73% of the living genera to which they were related also occur in the flora of present-day Indonesia. This strongly suggests that the London area at that time was in the vicinity of an Indonesian-type jungle flora, whereas today it would be (but for man's depredations) an area of temperate forest.

It is of great interest to know the nature of the coal-forests of the Palaeozoic Era. Many of its plants are extinct and it is not easy to make definite statements about their habitats. But it has been suggested, for instance, that the absence of tree-rings in certain of these fossils indicates a lack of seasonal variation, whereas plants now growing in regions where the fossils are found today prove in their ringed wood that the climate may have become more seasonal—though the Palaeozoic trees' incapacity to develop tree-rings could have arisen from their primitive stage in evolution.

That these coal-forests were truly forests is evident from the abundance of roots and other fossils associated with the coal. The black dusty carbon in the coal, which makes it so dirty, may possibly point to forest fires; the great height (often over 100 ft) of the trees speaks clearly of an adequate rainfall; but whether it was tropical or not is not so easy to decide. In this connection it is noteworthy that West Patagonia (cool, temperate, where glaciers encroach on the sea) is as densely forested at low levels as the Amazon basin (tropical rain-forest), and in Alaska forests have taken root on actual glaciers, nourished by the morainic débris lying on the ice.

FOSSIL ATTITUDES

One may sometimes make deductions from the attitudes in which organisms are fossilized. Upon finding a coal-seam, the geologist, knowing that coal is the compressed remains of vegetable matter, will look for the roots of the plants which have provided the coal. If he finds roots beneath the coal-seam striking directly down to the 'seat-earth', and connecting with the coal above, he can reasonably deduce that the coal is 'in situ'—that is, the trees died, rotted and were compressed were they fell. Some coals can, however, originate from transported plant material. 'Cannel coal' (which derives its name from canwyl: a candle, because it burns with a candle-like flame) is an example of this, and may contain fossil fish not to be found in normal coal and so presumably the cannel coal must, in at least some cases, have been formed in a lake, whereas the normal coal is formed by terrestrial or swampy peat. On the

Isle of Wight coast (England) there is a tangle of Cretaceous trees which have evidently been washed down a flooded river and stranded. They were buried and are now, as fossilized logs, being excavated by the sea.

Animal fossils, being smaller and more transportable than trees, are more commonly found away from their places of origin; in fact, apart from the corals, it is sometimes difficult to find an appreciable number of animal fossils in the same locality where their owners lived and died.

Fossils which have been transported do, however, convey information about the circumstances of their burial. Belemnites, for instance, often align themselves so that their long axes point roughly in a constant direction—this being the direction of the current which was prevalent at the time the belemnites were laid down and buried.

On looking closer at the fossils themselves, the expert can sometimes discern features which clarify the environment in which the creatures lived. This is particularly noticeable when considering the Bivalvia (i.e. the double-shelled molluscs—cockles, mussels, oysters, etc.). On the whole, three modes of life are pursued by the Bivalvia, and their characteristics are as follows:

MODE OF LIFE	GENERALISED CHARACTERISTICS
Active	teeth present inequilateral equivalve isomyarian
Sessile (cemented)	teeth feeble or absent equilateral inequivalve anisomyarian (unequal muscle scars) or monomyarian (one muscle scar)
Sessile (attached by a byssus)	teeth feeble or absent shell shape variable anisomyarian or monomyarian
Burrowing	teeth feeble or absent inequilateral equivalve anisomyarian or isomyarian

The terminology is explained in Fig. 9, where equilateral and inequilateral refer to the symmetry of the shell, equivalve and inequivalve to the similarity (or otherwise) of the two shells, and the terms ending in '-myarian' refer to the muscle-scars inside the shells. Bivalves characteristically have teeth, which are continuations of the shell and, in their form and function, are more like dovetail joints in woodwork than our teeth. These are to prevent the valves from being sheared apart by starfish and other causes, and have no feeding function. They also have muscles which pull the valves together for protection, and other purposes.

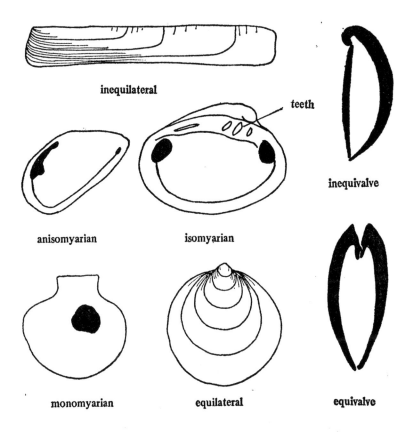

Fig. 9   *Some terms used in the Bivalvia*

The active bivalves live on the sea floor, or perhaps buried a little in the mud or sand, breathing water gently in and out again between the shells. Cemented bivalves (oysters and so on) are fixed in position and, like trees, corals, and other fixed objects, tend to grow equally in all directions: this leads to an equilateral habit, while the lid-on-a-box type of valve operation causes the upper valve to stay small while the lower fixed valve grows large (inequivalve condition). Some bivalves (mussels etc.) are fixed to rocks by a system of proteinous threads (byssus) like tent-guys. Such a bivalve may be asymmetrical when view from the side (i.e., inequilateral) because of the off-centre position of the byssus, though this is not always so. On the other hand, burrowing bivalves owe their inequilateral shape to the fact that streamlining is necessary for burrowing purposes.

One can deduce the environment of a fossil bivalve from its appearance. Sometimes the fossils of burrowers can be found in their own burrows. Cemented bivalves can sometimes be found where they lived, and if detached from the rock on which they were fixed, can, in favourable circumstances, reveal an impression of the rock on the scar of its attachment area. Additional information as to how far the shells have been transported is provided by their convex up/convex down and open/closed ratios. Water currents tend to flip bivalve shells over so that they lie convex up, this being a more streamlined position for them. Since muscles can only exert a closing action by contraction, opening of bivalve shells is effected by a non-living but elastic ligament, which operates on or near the hinge-line of the shell, and opens it when the muscles relax. When the creature dies the muscles rot, but the ligament is still operative and the valves open up. Thus the open/closed ratio of bivalve shells is an indication of how quickly the shell was buried; delayed burial allows the valves to become wide open when the muscles rot.

PAST AND PRESENT HABITATS

Guessing the habitat of an organism from a knowledge of its nearest present-day relatives, is a difficult task, and the difficulty is roughly proportional to the age of the fossil. Fossil species which are known as living organisms today are fairly easily treated, from this point of view, but few species alive today date back beyond the Pleistocene Period. From the Tertiary Era one often finds genera which are represented by species today, but the effort to establish how much a genus may have varied its surroundings, is fraught with pitfalls.

Let us consider the elephant. Today's elephants (*Elephas*—Indian elephant, and *Loxodonta*—African elephant) live in tropical environments, such as savanna and jungle. It would be reasonable to expect fossils of these species (*Elephas maximus* and *Loxodonta africana*) to be found in the same, or very similar, places. However, the fossil species include the mammoth, formerly known as *Elephas primigenius*—now *Mammuthus primigenius*—which lived in the Arctic tundra. Clearly, therefore, the genus *Elephas*, in its broad sense, has a wide-ranging habitat. Sometimes, of course, a species can change its ecological preferences: indeed, if this were not so, it would be difficult to visualize how evolution could take place. A famous example of this comes from the tiny water-snail, *Potamopyrgus jenkinsi*. Until the end of the nineteenth century this snail lived in estuaries; now it lives in fresh water. Such a change from brackish (i.e., salty, but less salty than the sea) to fresh water is remarkable in that it has happened within the span of the last century. Changes like these can affect many animal groups. Most sharks are marine, but can nevertheless also be found in certain non-marine areas—e.g. Lake Nicaragua. Likewise, the whales in the lakes of China have presumably swum up the rivers from the Pacific, while the robber crabs which climb trees in the Indopacific region, and will drown if deprived of air, and the diving beetles (insects being normally air-breathing) extend the record of anomalies beyond the vertebrates. With these anomalies in mind, however, it is possible, with the necessary background of knowledge, to infer an environment from the fossils thereof.

A classic example of the deduction of an environment from its fossils is the study of the mammals of the northern Great Basin (the high land in the American cordillera, north-east of California). Here about 20,000 fossils of mammals have been studied (the figure is of some significance since, in this kind of study, the more fossils that are available the better statistically will be the results obtained from them). There is a noticeable disappearance of the Perissodactyla (horse types), and a small invasion of Edentata (sloths etc.) in the Cenozoic strata. This last-mentioned phenomenon is a consequence of the reappearance of Panama as a continent-linking isthmus after a lengthy period (Eocene to Lower Pliocene) of isolation by water, of South from North America. Furthermore, the data show that there is a trend during the Tertiary Era, partially reversed in the Quaternary, towards a drying-out of the northern Great Basin, with a concomitant increase in the difference between the extremes of temperature. The general trend is from forest through savanna to grassland. Only the steam-bank community survived, in importance, throughout this period. The basic cause of this drying-out is, of course, another matter, but a plausible explanation is that the uplift of the mountains to the west caused a progressively more pronounced rain-shadow in the Great Basin, while the Quaternary reversal of this trend is no doubt a consequence of the general cooling and dampening of the climate during the ice ages.

OTHER EVIDENCE PROVIDED BY FOSSILS

On rare occasions it is possible to find fossils which by their actual appearance, tell us their cause of death. Near my home town of Portsmouth (England) some bones were recently found of Saxon men, evidently murdered, since one had a nail driven into his ear. Moving to the more remote past, one may quote the fish of the Rumanian Oligocene. Here the fish fossils show that the animals died with their mouths open, having apparently been asphyxiated through foul water conditions. It is interesting to notice that nearby is the Ploesti oilfield.

Fossil evidence for carnivorousness is unfortunately not often obvious, except indirectly, in the shape of the teeth. Teeth make excellent fossils (being hard and protected by highly resistant dentine), and they can be studied to tell the eating habits of the creatures owning them. Thus one may find the long, sharp teeth of the carnivore (shark, lion); the flat-crowned teeth of the herbivore (horse); the corrugated crushing teeth of the mollusc-eater (skate); and the pyramidical teeth of the insectivore (shrew). Many mammals, e.g. man, have a variety of teeth to cope with a varied diet. Only certain mammals, like the rodents, have continually growing teeth. In man, once the second set of teeth is formed, then, after that, any that are lost are lost then for good. This contrasts with the situation of the elephant; in addition to his tusks (which are modified teeth), new teeth continually form in his jaw so that as a tooth becomes worn out, a new one grows in its place. It is fascinating, though alas rare, to find actual toothmarks in a fossil, indicative of a violent death.

Habits other than those of feeding can sometimes be ascertained. Thus the presence of a tiny ichthyosaur skeleton within a large one indicates a viviparous birth for ichthyosaurs (marine reptiles of the Mesozoic Era)—that is, the young were formed within the parent and born alive, and not hatched through eggs.

Exceptionally well-preserved Palaeozoic cephalopods have been known to exhibit their original colouring on the fossil shells. On the assumption that (as is observably the case with the present-day Nautilus) the upper, sunlit side of the shell was gaily coloured while the lower side of the shell (which is seen by other creatures against the bright top-surface of the sea) is a plain, pale hue, it is clear that some of the Palaeozoic cephalopods swam with the apex directed horizontally, and some with it directed upwards. This conclusion accords with extraneous evidence of their swimming attitudes.

3   The Earliest Beginnings

'And God said, Let the waters generate' – John Milton, Paradise Lost

THE PRECAMBRIAN ATMOSPHERE

The origin of life is a problem whose solution is difficult and elusive. Clearly identifiable fossils begin in the Cambrian period. It is true there are fossils in the Precambrian rocks, but they are rare, often vaguely preserved, and it is generally difficult to correlate them with accepted classifications. Furthermore, even the simplest of Precambrian fossils can only provide evidence of life at a very early stage in the earth's history, and we are no nearer the actual origin of life than we would be to the origin of language by studying the oldest known literature of man.

There are clues, however, which, backed up with much reasonable, though admittedly conjectural, thought, can offer us an hypothesis. The first step in answering any questions like this is to decide where the clues are likely to be found, and in considering the origin of life, one must also consider the environment in which it evolved. Was the earth much warmer in the Precambrian Era or was it weighed down by glaciers? Was there an abundance of volcanoes? Did the seas cover all the land-surface? Was the sea salty? Was the atmosphere as it is now? These are weighty questions indeed, and I will only discuss the last one.

A science fiction story has been written about a time in the future when, as a result of a nuclear war, the earth has moved into a more elliptical orbit than it has now, so that every time it passed close to the sun, some air was lost to the sun's gravity, and thus the earth's atmosphere gradually rarified. The survivors of the war slowly asphyxiated. This, of course, is a mere fantasy, but geological data present us with evidence of an equally unbreathable atmosphere in the past.

Certain Precambrian gravels are known, presumably deposited by water (and with the atmosphere being either directly in contact with the gravel or as gases dissolved in the water), whose contents differs from those of today's gravels. The difference lies in the mineralogy : quartz grains are present in both, but whereas modern gravels may contain iron oxides the ancient gravel contains pyrite (iron sulphide) which was evidently conveyed by the water as sand-sized grains, to its present position. Now, pyrite is moderately stable in our present atmosphere, but it is nowadays not laid down in the presence of aerated water, since the oxygen in the air and water encourages the formation of iron oxides rather than sulphides. The ancient gravel, then, must have been formed in deoxygenated water. Deoxygenated water can still occur in stagnant conditions, but running water (such as would form gravel) inevitably absorbs air on its course, and so pyrite-bearing gravels suggest an oxygen-free atmosphere.

The concept of an oxygen-free atmosphere has important implications apart from the inability of animals to breathe it. The stratosphere, which lies above the atmosphere at a height of $5\frac{1}{2}$–11 miles or more, contains a zone of ozone (a form of oxygen) which, though very rarified, is of cardinal importance to us in that it shields us from the lethal ultraviolet rays constantly being emitted by the sun. Some ultraviolet gets through, it is true, and causes us to become suntanned, but if it were all allowed to enter the lower atmosphere, we should be burned to death in a very short time This layer of ozone is produced from the oxygen in the atmosphere, and an oxygen-free atmosphere would, then, be open to the ultraviolet rays.

This leads to a paradox : if ultraviolet rays are lethal, and if there was no oxygen to breathe, how could life, as we know it, have existed? The answer is twofold. Firstly, anaerobic (non-oxygen breathing) life is well known, even now; certain environments are often rich in anaerobic bacteria which live on compounds containing oxygen in the combined state only (e.g. sulphates). Secondly, ultraviolet light, though lethal to us, is a powerful promoter of chemical reactions. Experiments have been carried out with ultraviolet light and electrical discharges (which could occur naturally as lightning) and it has been found that these agencies promote the formation of quite complicated organic molecules from simple inorganic beginnings (carbon dioxide, water etc.). Admittedly, no one has yet created life in this fashion, but in the immensity of geological time life might well have been created by these natural processes acting on naturally-occurring chemicals. The next step would be the release of free oxygen from its combined state, as plants do to this day in photosynthesis; probably by the action of algae (simple plants and seaweeds) or algae-like organisms, which would in turn provide the ozone to protect the earth from the ultraviolet rays. Continued cut-off of the ultraviolet could lead to the development of life which was incapable of withstanding the ultraviolet which its ancestors received.

The question remains: when did all this happen? Dating of non-fossiliferous rocks is notoriously difficult, but the rocks bearing evidence of an oxygen-free atmosphere seem to give place to rocks of a more recent type at about 1,000–2,000 million years ago. This is roughly three times as long ago as the Cambrian Period, and may itself be a milestone of importance in that it marks the boundary between anaerobic and aerobic life as a dominant feature of this planet.

PRECAMBRIAN FOSSILS

Before considering the Cambrian Period and its rich and varied fossils (compared with those of the Precambrian), it is necessary to consider Precambrian fossils as far as they are known. These fossils may be of the actual organisms themselves, or provide indirect evidence of the activities of organisms which have not actually fossilized themselves. The indirect evidence includes certain limestone formations which have so far been considered to be most plausibly explained as the work of algae or alga-like organisms. These 'algal' limestones date back to the early Precambrian— specimens from Rhodesia being reputedly 3,000 million years old— and extend into the lower Palaeozoic system.

Of the more convincing fossils of actual organisms, those of the Gunflint iron formation of Canada are of special interest in view of their great age (dating is very difficult, but between 1,000 and 2,000 million years seems likely) and their excellent state of preservation. The fossils are of simple microscopic plants, silicified during fossilization (i.e. replaced or impregnated by silica). Some of these fossils look like algae, and some like fungi. If they do include true algae then we can assume that photosynthesis was practised by these plants and carbon dioxide was being broken down to free oxygen, thus supplying the ingredient necessary for animal life.

Not quite so old as the Gunflint plants, but a good deal more varied, are the fossils from the Precambrian rocks of the Ediacara area, in Australia. Unlike the Gunflint fossils, the Australian fossils are impressions of soft-bodied animals plainly visible to the naked eye. The creatures seem to have lived on shallow-water mudflats which were covered with sand; the sand has hardened to form a hard sandstone or quartzite, which, when blocks of it fall off the cliffs of the Ediacara hills, loses the muddy material (now in the form of sericite, a micaceous substance which, though harder than mud, is still soft enough to weather away easily) and so reveals

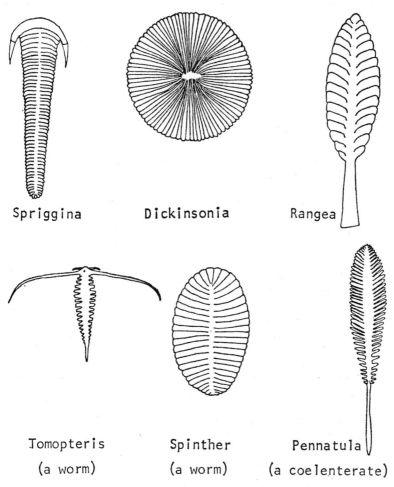

Spriggina   Dickinsonia   Rangea

Tomopteris   Spinther   Pennatula
(a worm)   (a worm)   (a coelenterate)

Fig. 10 *Precambrian fossils and some modern creatures
which resemble them*
(not to scale)

the fossils as impressions in the quartzite. The Ediacara fossils can only be described as peculiar: some resemble jellyfish and others resemble polyp-like creatures; some look like annelid worms, and some are completely unrecognizable in terms of any known organism. None can be, with any confidence, closely related to any animal groups, but certain analogies are possible. See Fig. 10, and in this diagram the Precambrian fossils (*Dickinsonia*, *Spriggina*, *Rangea*) are to be compared with the present-day creatures shown below them. It is also noteworthy that the 'annelid worms' of Ediacara e.g. *Spriggina*, appear similar to both the annelid worms of today and the primitive trilobites of the Lower Cambrian.

THE TRANSITION TO THE CAMBRIAN

In the Cambrian Period, fossils begin to occur in sufficient quantities for anyone studying that period in any part of the world, to have a reasonable chance of finding fossils. True, the Lower Cambrian is often rather poor in its fossil complement, but a rich and diversified fauna has been obtained by intensive collecting throughout the world, whereas the Precambrian rocks lying immediately below the Cambrian generally yield a fauna of precisely nothing. The difference between the Cambrian and Precambrian fauna is not merely one of abundance, however. Whereas the fossils of Ediacara (and other Precambrian localities) are of soft-bodied creatures, whose only hard parts are tiny bristles or spicules (diminutive spikes built into the soft parts to make them firmer), the Cambrian Period immediately contains hard-shelled fossils. There were, of course, soft-bodied worms and such-like in the Cambrian Period, but their fossils are scarce and insignificant compared with the hard, shelly fossils. A further distinction to note between the Cambrian and Precambrian fossils is that whereas the latter are rather 'queer' and difficult to relate to modern groups, the Cambrian fossils are often easily related to groups of today. Indeed all major groups of fossilizable organisms (except the Bryozoa and vertebrates) can be traced back to the Cambrian Period (see Fig. 11).

What was the cause of this extraordinary increase in the fossil record? The rocks containing the Ediacara fossils do not seem to be markedly different from the rocks containing the Cambrian fossils. It may be that the dawn of the Cambrian was the dawn of hard-shell creations, but it is difficult to see why so many independent groups of animals developed hard shells, more or less at once, in the Lower Cambrian, unless perhaps one group 'invented' the carnivorous mode of life, thus obliging other groups to follow suit.

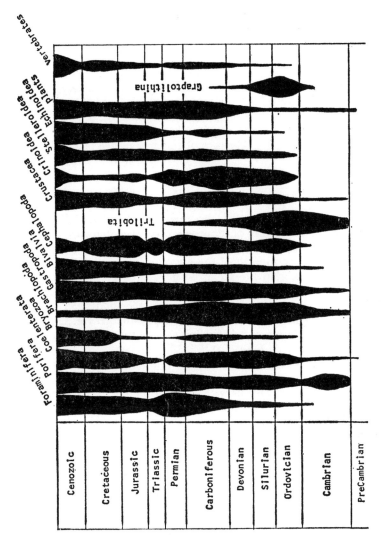

Fig. 11 *History of the major groups of fossils*

Alternatively, it may be that the oxygenic atmosphere evolved slowly, and that Precambrian animal-life existed in tiny, sparsely-distributed groups where there was sufficient plant life, and unable to exist elsewhere because scant plant life would mean a small oxygen output, which would combine very quickly with iron and other chemicals in the Precambrian sea. The dawn of the Cambrian could be, in this view, the beginning of a period when there was enough oxygen in the sea to complete the oxidation of reactive chemicals in solution, and still leave enough dissolved oxygen in the water to enable animal life to spread unhindered through the oceans. A threshold, where the oxygen content of the sea suddenly increased to more than was required by the oxidizable chemicals in it, could explain the suddenness of the appearance of Cambrian life.

LIFE IN THE CAMBRIAN

Whatever the explanation of the origin of Cambrian life, the evidence of the abundance of its widely diversified and structurally quite advanced animal groups, indicates that there is a long Precambrian history to most of these groups, could we but find it. Furthermore, Cambrian life seems to have been restricted to the sea, and indeed it was not till the Silurian and Devonian periods that life began to venture from the sea into the inhospitable non-marine world, which harboured such dangers as winter ice, summer drought, swift currents, varying salinities, and the strange environments of air and land.

It would be as well to review here some of the fossil groups represented in the Cambrian, and, though it is perhaps a little annoying that life presents us with a 'fait accompli' in that most of the major groups were already established in the early Cambrian record, we can draw comfort from the knowledge that the Cambrian Period was a time of early experimentation, and that many of the Cambrian sub-groups ultimately became extinct or very scarce, whereas the succeeding Ordovician Period saw the establishment of many sub-groups which are still extant today, and are thus less exotic by present-day standards.

The Cambrian fauna is as follows:

Kingdom Plantae (plants): algal or algal-like limestones represent the plants. Some of these structures are also to be found in the Precambrian

Kingdom Protista: these are one-celled organisms, Protozoa and the like, whose properties fall between those of true plants and those of true animals. The tiny skeletons of these creatures are known from the Cambrian.

Kingdom Animalia (animals):

Phylum Brachiopoda : these bivalve-like creatures are still a living group today, though sadly reduced in numbers compared with the past. They are common fossils in the Cambrian.

Phylum Arthropoda (insects, etc.): Class Trilobita : very common in the Cambrian. Extinct after the Palaezoic Era.

rest of Phylum : representatives are known, but they are not common.

Phylum Mollusca: primitive members of this group are known, rather scantily, from the Cambrian

Phylum Echinodermata (starfish etc.): early members of this Phylum are known in the Cambrian

Phylum Porifera (sponges): these occur in the Cambrian

Phylum Chordata (vertebrates and related groups): vertebrate remains are not known till the Ordovician Period, but if the graptolites are indeed (as has been suggested) related to, or part of, this phylum, then it can be considered to begin in the Cambrian. Certain bizarre fossils grouped under the name of Calcichordata (see p. 54), which have been assigned to the Chordata, also occur in this period.

Phylum Coelenterata : jellyfish, considering their softness, have a remarkably long fossil record, extending back to the Cambrian and Precambrian. Corals on the whole begin in the Ordovician, but their beginnings are discernible in the Cambrian

Fig. 12 shows these data diagrammatically, the thickness of the black columns representing the number of fossils to be found.

Clearly, therefore, the overall pattern of the living world had been roughly established in the Cambrian Period, including the major groups of the animal world (phyla), though the classes within these phyla are rather unfamiliar to our eyes. The extent of this unfamiliarity is nowhere more striking than in the Middle Cambrian fauna of the Burgess Shale.

The circumstances of the discovery of the remarkable Burgess Shale fossils are quoted here from A. Lee MacAlester's book, *The History of Life* (Prentice-Hall).

'While crossing a steep mountain pass near Field, British Columbia, Walcott and his party stumbled on some slabs of dark shale containing both Middle Cambrian trilobites and clear impressions of soft-bodied, worm-like fossils. Investigation revealed that the fossils occurred in several poorly exposed shale layers on the steep slope of the pass. In the following summers Walcott returned

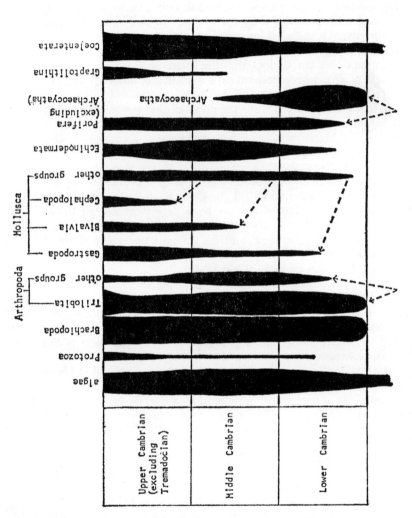

Fig. 12   *Cambrian life: the history of the major fossil groups*

to the locality with a large field party that blasted and quarried 22 feet into solid rock to collect the fossils, most of which were found in a single three-foot layer. Preliminary studies by Walcott revealed that the fauna contained over 100 species of well-preserved soft-bodied invertebrates in addition to many shell-bearing trilobites and sponges ... it is dominated by arthropods, both trilobites and unique representatives of four primitive non-shelled classes.'

One reads with envy of people stumbling on fossils like these. The arthropods certainly exhibit an extraordinary variety of types showing that the diversity of this phylum was widespread even in the earliest stages of fossil history. Fig. 13 shows four Burgess shale fossils selected more or less at random to show the variety of forms present.

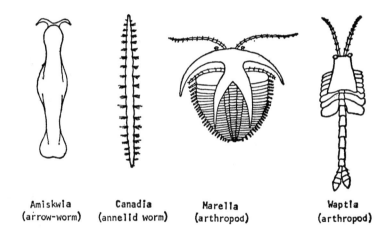

Amiskwia   Canadia   Marella   Waptia
(arrow-worm)   (annelid worm)   (arthropod)   (arthropod)

Fig. 13   *Burgess shale fossils (middle cambrian)*

Trilobites, which range through the Palaeozoic Era, are now an extinct group, but in the Cambrian and Ordovician Periods they exhibited a great diversity and a widespread occurrence comparable with that of modern crabs. Particularly remarkable are the trilobites' eyes, which, though rudimentary or absent, are sometimes compound like a fly's eye and presumably, apart from the fact that the trilobites lived under water, gave a similar picture of the world to that seen by the present-day fly.

The Cambrian rocks are rich in mysterious shells whose affinities are very uncertain. Among these are the calyptoptomatids, a group of conical calcareous shells which sometimes show evidence of dividing-plates inside, and even fin-like structures outside the shell. An operculum (lid) is also sometimes to be found. These shells are common in the marine Cambrian shales, but their position in the animal kingdom is very vague. Other conical shells are known from the Cambrian Period—some of them are calcareous, while others, which are phosphatic, can be etched out of the surrounding lime-stone with acid. It is often easier to know the modes of life of the creatures responsible for these shells than it is to know what they actually were.

4   Life in the Sea

'Learn of the little Nautilus to sail,
Spread the thin oar, and catch the driving gale'
                                                — *Pope*

REEF AND LAGOON LIFE

Those who live near the coral seas—the Red Sea, the Indian Ocean,
the Caribbean, and the South and West Pacific—are privileged to
see the marine life of today's world at its height. In many ways the
terrestrial life of our planet seems to be in decline, but as far as
the oceans are concerned life is still flourishing. The Great Barrier
Reef of Australia (1,000 miles long and 15–180 miles wide, and made
up largely of coral and algal rock) is enormous by any standards,
past or present. Moreover, in addition to mere size, the reefs are
rich in a great variety of life, from small burrowing bivalves which
bore their way into the coral rock, through the organisms which
grow and crawl on the surface (seaweeds, corals, starfish, sea-
urchins, gastropods, bivalves), to the swimming fish and drifting
plankton which are linked indirectly with the reef by food, reproduction, and other invisible chains.

It is a significant fact that much of the so-called 'coral' reefs of
today is composed of non-coral material: about half the reef is
commonly the product of algae (seaweeds, etc.). Furthermore, the
reefs of the ancient past often had an even lower proportion of
coral material in them, the corals sometimes being mere adventitious
organisms on the surface of the reef, like trees in a savanna; or
there might, in some cases, have been no true corals on the reef
at all. One might well ask, what then *is* a reef? It has been suggested
that the name derived from the Old Norse *rif* (a chain of rocks),
and, in later times, came to mean any hard ridge reaching, or not
much below, the surface of the sea, often formed by corals. In the
context of this book, the term 'reef' will be taken to mean any
large mass of rock formed *in situ* under water by living organisms.
The term *in situ* implies the exclusion of shell-banks composed of
shells washed up by waves or currents from other localities.

For the purpose of illustrating various types of reef, a few examples will be taken from the fossil record—the Canadian Silurian, the British Permian, the German Jurassic—and these will be compared with modern reefs.

The Niagaran (Silurian) series of rocks in Canada afford an excellent example of the Palaeozoic reefs which are also to be found in rocks of a similar age in Britain, Sweden, and elsewhere. The Niagaran reefs of the Great Lakes area have evidently been developed on a soft Silurian sea-floor, probably beginning as tentative calcareous incrustations on shells and other hard objects and later spreading to form their own solid bases for further growth. Evidently the marine conditions became favourable for reef-formation in the Middle Silurian times, and ceased being so later on. The first phase in the reef-construction, where it is visible, seems to have been conducted in relatively deep water, and consists mainly of a strongly-built colonial type of coral now extinct (tabulate type). A little later the class, Stromatoporoidea, which is extinct today, but belongs to the same phylum (Coelenterata) as the corals, played an important part when the the reef was built up to a level of incipient wave-action, and the corals became less important.

Stromatoporoid fossils have a variable shape; often hard, compact, calcareous structures and sometimes the size of a man's fist, a football, or even larger. They have a complicated microstructure and evidently housed colonies of polyp-creatures when alive, rather like modern colonial corals. These stromatoporoids, along with certain other fossils, provided the first wave-resistant reefs of the Niagara rocks, which in turn, in their capacity as hard, upstanding parts of the sea floor, were favoured for further reef-formation, the water evidently being shallower and rougher in this intermediate phase. In the final phase further reef-formation occurred and stromatoporoids continued to do much of the actual work of building the reef. But on the submarine surface of the reef a great variety of life swarmed—trilobites, molluscs, sponges, and many less familiar organisms are preserved for us in great profusion.

A block of Middle Silurian Wenlock reef-limestone from England, formed under very similar conditions to those of the later stages of the Middle Silurian Niagara reefs of Canada just described shows:

Phylum Brachiopoda : these are represented by many shells, some being, no doubt, in their position of life, though most are drifted-in by currents.

Phylum Bryozoa : plentiful.

Phylum Arthropoda : some fragments of trilobite shells are to be seen.

Phylum Mollusca : these are still scarce, but both gastropods and bivalves are recognizable, and the phylum is becoming less rare as the Palaeozoic era proceeds.

Phylum Echinodermata : the phylum is richly represented by the crinoids, which—though they often leave only their stems as fossils—are commonplace in the Palaeozoic rocks.

Phylum Porifera : remains are known from these rocks.

Phylum Chordata : fish remains are rare so early in the Silurian, but graptolites are still commonplace (though dying out by now).

When these reefs reached an advanced stage, and had grown so high as to show evidence in the rocks and the broken fossils associated with them, of the shallow, rough water, they seemed to 'die'—that is, no further reef-formation took place. Forests of crinoids thronged their top surfaces, and today masses of crinoid stems are often to be found just above the reefs. The surrounding sediments silted over them, and the crinoids were buried and fossilized to become, like the termite hills, mute reminders of the teeming life that formerly was concentrated in and on them.

In North America, where the Middle Silurian reefs can be seen to curve in a great V-shape with the apex of the V in the Central U.S.A., and the arms reaching up to the islands of the Canadian Arctic and Labrador, it seems that the reefs may possibly owe their distribution to the waves and currents of the time, which may in fact have been dominated by the prevailing winds (which would, of course, have been very different from the winds of today). In England the reefs seem to be associated with the Midland block, which was shallow water at that time, and the Welsh area, which was deep-water and hence poorer in limestones. The boundary between these two areas appears to be strongly faulted, and this faulting action, with its tendency to create areas of persistent uplift and subsidence, may have affected the formation of the reefs.

On the Isle of Oesel in the Baltic, late-Silurian deposits contain relatively good fish fossils in the non-marine parts and fragmentary —probably derived—fish remains in the marine parts. Earlier fish remains have been reported from the Russian and North American Ordovician; the American fossils are fragmentary and worn and seem to have been transported from a nearby landmass. Apparently the fish, unlike most animals, began as non-marine creatures which subsequently diversified into the sea. One has to say 'apparently' since we know very little of the fishes' ancestry, and until we do we will not know whether the fossils of fish found so far are the earliest fish.

A clue towards the answer, is to be found in the Cambrian, Ordovician, Silurian and Devonian rocks. Amongst the fossils of these rocks are to be found the remains of various creatures which, though having calcite skeletons and stem-plates of the echinoderm type, possess other features which are very strange in the echinoderm concept. Jeffries, in 1967, has shown how these last-mentioned characteristics can be compared with the anatomy of fish and has proposed that these fossils be moved into a new subphylum, the Calcichordata (see Fig. 14), and that they be classified as members of the Phylum Chordata. Thus, by all appearances, the vertebrates are related to the starfish phylum through these strange little fossils in the Lower Palaeozoic. Perhaps it might even be true to say that the Calcichordata are actually ancestral to the vertebrates. Fig. 14 shows *Cothurnocystis*, a member of the Calcichordata, with its calcite plates and U-shaped slits, together with a reconstruction of its hypothetical living position—it is assumed to be bottom-dwelling because, like the flatfish, it is a flat creature. If the slits are indeed homologous with a fish's gill-slits, there must indeed be some connection with the vertebrates here. The whole problem of the origin of the vertebrates is fraught with difficulties and it is hard enough to decide to what extent living forms like the acorn-worms, baglike sea-squirts, spineless lancet-fish, or polyp-bearing pterobranchs are truly related to the original developers of the backbone without introducing extinct links like the Calcichordata and graptolites.

If we consider another Palaeozoic Period, the Permian, we can, as usual, choose several places in the world to study its reefs. The biggest Permian reef is that of the Texas/New Mexico area. Here, the understanding of the controversial geology of the area was frustrated by difficulties of interpreting the evidence of the fossils. At the other end of the world, the Indonesian island of Timor has become famous in palaeontology for its rich fossil record in the Permian and Triassic Periods. Marine life apparently abounded there as it does today, and indeed the similarity is heightened by the occasional presence of volcanic ash with the fossils.

In northern Europe, in the Permian Period, an arm of what appears to have been a forerunner of the Arctic Ocean, reached down from East Greenland to Britain and Germany. This Zechstein Sea, as it is called, must have been very warm for the reef-bearing limestones to be found in Britain are succeeded, as the sea receded from the British shores, by salts marking an evaporation phase. Much of Britain was at this time in the grip of a desert climate and the conditions must have been somewhat analogous to that of Aden today. Furthermore, it can be seen from the fossil content

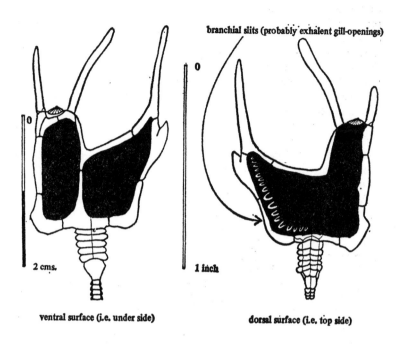

branchial slits (probably exhalent gill-openings)

0

0

2 cms.

1 inch

ventral surface (i.e. under side)

dorsal surface (i.e. top side)

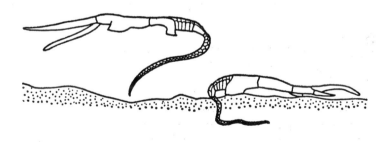

inferred living appearance

Fig. 14   *Cothurnocystis: a member of the Calcichordata*

of these reefs that a progressive restriction of the fauna took place as the Zechstein Sea slowly dried up. The variety of life wanes towards the top of the limestones: molluscs, a group more capable of accommodating to changes of salinity than the superficially-similar brachiopods, take over from the latter in importance. In the latest rocks, even the most resistant organisms disappear, and arid salt, marl, and sand deposits become the rule. One can visualize a succession of events: from a warm sea with reefs rich in life—brachiopods, molluscs, bryozoans, algae, and so on—through inter-mediate stages to a final recession of the sea, with impermanent lagoons inhabited only by the most resistant invertebrates, and finally lifeless salt-pans and deserts. These events took place several times before the Zechstein Sea finally disappeared from the British scene.

A study of the fossils in the quarries and cliffs which expose the Jurassic reefs, reveals a profound change in the fossil complement of the reef faunas. Corals are in that period more important than in the Palaeozoic Era, both as reef-builders and reef-users: molluscs are more numerous and echinoids have become more commonplace while crinoids have become scarcer. Trilobites are, of course, extinct by now. Sponges sometimes make a major contribution to the reef fauna. In Bavaria (Germany) certain of these Upper Jurassic rocks include lagoonal deposits in the form of 'lithographic limestone'. The limestone, because of its even-textured surface, was formerly used to make printing blocks for transferring the ink to paper—hence the term lithographic. The technique of printing is still some-times called lithography.

The lithographic limestone is famous for the beautifully-preserved fossils to be found therein, evidently belonging to creatures which fell into very calm water and were buried in sediment which was free from the usual agitation by currents, waves, crabs, mud-eating worms, and so forth. Of the Phylum Coelenterata, true jellyfish can be seen as imprints in the limestone; perhaps the jellyfish were stranded by the outgoing tide. There is also an excellently-preserved marine worm, *Eunicites*, which is not only preserved as an impres-sion in outline, like a silhouette, but also shows the bristly parts in its sides and the little hard jaws at the end of the mouth. In the same area, 'ropes' of castings have been found, presumably thrown out of a burrowing worm's body, like the sandy 'ropes' along the sea-shore today.

Of the shelly creatures there are numerous examples in the lithographic limestone. One of these is a belemnoid (an extinct, squid-like creature) which not only has preserved the reduced

equivalent of the hard, bullet-shaped internal skeleton (see Fig. 8),
but also the ink-sac. Around it is the outline of the soft parts,
which include the ten hook-studded arms. This ink-sac seems to be
characteristic of the octopus-squid-cuttlefish group of cephalopods
to which the belemnoid-creatures belonged, and it is so well preserved in fossils like those of the lithographic limestone that it can
be moistened and used as ink again even at the present time.
Another remarkable record, in these lagoons, of the cephalopod
world is provided by the ammonites. One of the ammonites has
left the mark of its circumference in the limestone, and nearby
the impression of the side of the ammonite can be seen where it
fell over in the shallows, and on it lies the ammonite itself. This
shows how the ammonites, as had long been suspected from the
hydrostatics of the ammonite shell, swam body-lowermost with
the shell disposed vertically, like a cartwheel, the empty chambers
buoying the shell into this position. Ammonites only fell on to one
side, it seems, when they came to rest on the sea-floor. (The living
nautiloid *Nautilus* swims in a similarly upright fashion.)

The most famous of the fossils of the lithographic limestone,
however is *Archaeopteryx*, the bird-reptile known only from two
individual specimens, both found in this limestone. These strange
creatures, toothed like reptiles but feathered like birds, evidently
died in or near the lagoon and were preserved in their totality in
the lagoonal mud, now a limestone. (See Chapter 2 for a discussion
of their palaeontological significance.)

In addition to the fossils described above, well-preserved bugs,
moths, dragonflies (some of large size), beetles and stick-insects are
found represented by more or less recognizable Jurassic versions in
the limestone. Lobsters and king-crabs, some so well-preserved that
they look ready to crawl out of the rock, have been found. The
faunal lists are so long for this rock that they bring to life a vision
of this corner of Germany as it was then: a calm lagoon, a warm
landscape, and not far off the waves breaking on the reefs; insects
in the air (some looking a little strange and primitive, perhaps, but
mostly recognizable as belonging to present-day groups), with
Archaeopteryx flopping and gliding through the trees; tall ferns,
conifers, and cycad-type plants; lobsters in the pools by the lagoon;
ammonites, belemnoids, and Mesozoic fish (the latter studded with
glittering, enamelled scales) swimming in the sunlit water, while
beyond the reefs lies the open German sea. There would, however,
be virtually no mammals (except the ambiguous mamal-like reptiles)
in evidence, no true birds other than *Archaeopteryx*, no grass and
no flowers: a silent and monotonous world, broken only by the

grunts of the reptiles and the modest colours of the vegetation. Perhaps *Archaeopteryx* could sing, but with a beakful of teeth such as it possessed, it does not seem likely.

We shall now consider the reefs of the present day. Their properties, especially of 'coral reefs', are fairly limited: water temperatures generally vary around 25°–29° C (lower temperatures are sometimes possible) and a firm sea-floor is preferable for the reef-building creatures to build on. Currents in the sea (to provide plankton, as food, for the coral polyps) and sunlight (to enable the algae, living symbiotically within the polyps' tissues, to produce their starch) are other requirements—the sunlight proviso means, in effect, that depths over 300 ft are too dark for reef-growth, and actually reef-corals thrive best down to about 100 ft depth. The water must be clear and free from any markedly abnormal salinities.

Of course, there are many non-reef corals and these can occur at great depths and widely-ranging temperatures. But, restricting our attention to reef-corals, we may observe that the above-mentioned requirements usually apply. Corals are not the only reef-builders; algae are important limestone formers and corals may take second place to them, or even be altogether absent. But generally speaking corals are the normal building-agents of most of today's reefs.

Other coelenterates, dismissed by non-specialists as 'coral', include horny corals (*Gorgonia*), staghorn coral (*Acropora*), organ-pipe coral (*Tubipora*), and so on. The porous limestone is soon bored into by a host of associated reef organisms—worms, bivalves, crabs, anemones—and sea-urchins nestle in hollows, their bristling spines pointing like spears towards anything that casts a shadow on their sensitive bodies. Crinoids still live on reefs, though less prominently so than in the past; the brachiopods have retired to a humble existence in less crowded waters, while the molluscs have developed greatly, perhaps at the brachiopods' expense. The ammonites and belemnoids are now gone, of course, but the fish are still there, though few mammals care for the reef environment.

CENTRAL AMERICA AS A LINK AND BARRIER TO SEA-LIFE

One would expect, of course, a profound difference between the faunas of the Caribbean and the tropical Pacific, since it is as much an undertaking for the gastropod or starfish to spread from one side of central America (hereinafter referred to as 'Panama') to the other (via Cape Horn or the Arctic Ocean), as it is for a lizard to spread from India to China via the Himalayas. Yet the genera of some animal groups, including the crabs and echinoderms, show a great degree of similarity between the Atlantic and Pacific sides of Panama. This idiosyncrasy of distribution is heightened by a study of the species, for here it is seen that there is only a small resemblance between the species east and west of Panama. Since most modern species of crabs and echinoderms cannot spread through the climatic zones of the southern route round the South American continent, it would seem likely that the resemblance of the East and West central American genera are due to the fact that Panama was flooded some time in the past. The genera spread across the flooded isthmus, and when the isthmus emerged from the water the genera remained the same on both sides of it, though new species evolved on each side which were distinct (new species take less time to evolve than new genera). Significantly, species which *are* mutual to both sides of the isthmus today are ancient types, as old as the isthmus itself; and many species are 'twin species', i.e. closely related (the species having only just become distinct). These observations are to some extent also true of the fish and molluscs.

It has thus been possible, on the basis of recent data alone, to conclude that Panama was once flooded. Geological evidence supports this, and we know that South America was cut off from North America by a shallow sea during the Eocene, Oligocene, Miocene and Lower Pliocene periods. This explains the emergence of a strange, isolated land fauna in the South American Tertiary Era, which was suddenly invaded from the north in the Upper Pliocene Period. As it is commonly true of invasions from large areas to small ones (North America in this case belongs to Eurasia/Africa by virtue of the frequently dried-up Bering Straits), most of the survivors of the interchange were from the large area. In the case of Panama, the sabre-tooth, mastodon, raccoons, horses, peccaries, mice, and deer invaded from the north; sloths and armadillos crept up from the south.

It is intriguing to speculate as to what might happen if the isthmus of Suez was to disappear beneath the waves. The rich, varied marine life of the Indian Ocean would then be free to invade the Mediterranean via the Red Sea, and large, brilliantly-coloured molluscs and corals would spread northwards. The Mediterranean, on the other hand, is an almost landlocked lake; its fauna is humble and scanty compared with the exotica of the Far East. A submerged Suez, therefore, would promote the inflow of life into the Mediterranean, with a lesser exchange the other way.

LIFE IN THE DEEP SEA

The sea can be roughly divided into three regions—the shelf
(0–600 ft deep, approx.), the slope (600 ft–10,000 ft, approx.), and
the abyss (10,000 ft–36,000 ft, approx.). This threefold division is
due to the fact that the edges of the continents, as we see them, are
seldom the true edges; these are to be found under about 600 ft of
water, and beyond these edges the earth's profile slopes relatively
steeply into the abyss, a region where huge plains are scarred with
deep clefts and studded with underwater hills and mountains (see
Fig. 15).

The shelf holds most of the life of the ocean; sunlight is able to
penetrate about 300 ft of water (that is, under favourable conditions
for towards the poles the turbidity in the water and the low angle
of incidence of the sun's rays reduces the degree of penetration),
and in this region seaweeds, algae and corals flourish. The plant-
plankton and animal-plankton drift in these illuminated regions,
the latter for the sake of plant-food. Also benthic (bottom-dwelling)

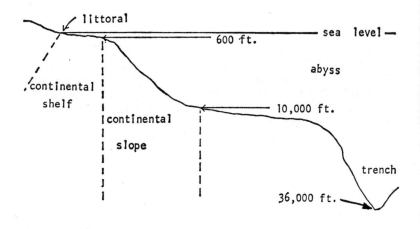

Fig. 15   *Faunal regions in the sea*

life abounds: crabs, lobsters, molluscs, star-fish, sea-urchins. At 600 ft life is scarcer, and the light, if any, is a deep, cold-blue colour. Below 600 ft currents are few, temperatures are low, and darkness prevails. The sea-floor is muddy and soft, and few animals care to venture into these depths. In the depths of the abyss, 10,000 ft–20,000 ft or more there are muds and oozes, and the water is very cold—meltwater from the polar regions sinks because of its high density and flows over the ocean floors, reducing temperatures to 4° C or thereabouts, even at the equator.

Sedimentation may be very slow (the rivers deposit most of their material on or near the shelf); meteoric dust and windborne volcanic ash occur, sharks' teeth lie unburied for centuries. Multitudes of mineral nodules occur in patches on the sea-floor. Oozes, the accumulated product of disintegration of millions of planktonic organisms, accumulate slowly. In this realm of blackness a few quaint creatures grope their way; mostly blind, they may be a sickly white or black, or strangely enough, even bright red in colour. Their flabby tissues are ill-adapted to powerful muscular action. Hideous fish with huge jaws and needle-like teeth wait for their prey to blunder into them. This is a realm which, though known to oceanograpical surveys, is little-known to geology. Few fossils can definitely be attributed to the abyss; either the abyssal rocks are very unfossiliferous or one does not find them raised frequently enough to be commonly visible on land.

THE MOLLUSCS

The molluscs, like the vertebrates, have invaded virtually every habitat available to them. There are land, lake, river, and sea molluscs. Some snails can survive desert drought, some slugs can burrow deep into the soil, some bivalves bore into hard limestone. There are no flying molluscs, however, unless one includes the flying squids which skim over the waves very much like the flying fish. There are probably more species of molluscs, alive and fossilized, than any other group of animals, apart from the arthropods (insects, spiders, crabs etc.). Molluscs have also been prized by man—4,000 shells of cowries (*Cypraea moneta*) were valued at one English shilling in Victorian India. A string of 25–40 tusk-shells (*Dentalium indianorum*) were worth one slave in North-West Canada. Shells were cut up to make wampum in North America, and knives and fishhooks in the Pacific. *Pinctada*, the pearl-oyster, has, for centuries, provided pearls and nacre; *Ostrea*, the edible oyster, has been a source of food since the Stone Age.

Palaeontology shows that molluscs, like most animals, first appear in the Cambrian Period, and clearly show their modern diversification into groups, in the Ordovician Period. Also, following the normal pattern, they show a deployment, from marine to non-marine environments, in the Devonian and later periods.

If one considers the three principal types of molluscs (see Fig. 16), one can see little in the way of a common denominator. Gastropods are mostly helically coiled, cephalopods are mostly with internal shells (though flat spirals of the ammonoids and nautiloids, which contain the soft parts within them, were dominant in the past), and bivalves are, of course, bivalve. A study of the primitive members of living molluscs, along with a study of the embryonic history of certain members of the phylum, has suggested for a long time that the original mollusc must have resembled the hypothetical 'Archaetype'—that is, a creature with only basic, unmodified organs and a cap-shaped shell. It is of much interest to the specialist in living mollusc zoology to enquire of the palaeontologists whether a mollusc of this type has been found as a fossil.

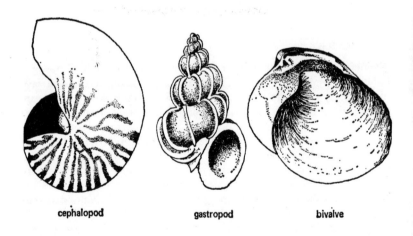

cephalopod   gastropod   bivalve

Fig. 16   *Molluscs*

Until recently it was difficult to answer yes or no to this question. The oldest known cephalopod (Upper Cambrian) had curved shells and the usual cephalopod structure—septa (horizontal compartments) and siphuncle (connections between the compartments). The earliest bivalves are Middle Cambrian. The earliest gastropods (Cambrian), however, not only included the 'normal' snail types (helical shell), but also cap-shaped 'limpets', some of which are known to be alive and thriving today. The limpets of today, of course, are not particularly primitive, being merely coiled gastropods which have secondarily uncoiled their shells. Many show this by being coiled in the early part of their life. But how about the Cambrian limpets? Were they at the truly primitive pre-helical stage? It is curious that, whereas some Cambrian gastropods are helically coiled, many are limpet-shaped. It is none too easy to determine whether the soft body of the Cambrian limpets was coiled or not, but the careful study of muscle-scars on well-preserved specimens indicates that, in at least some instances, the body was in a pre-coiled condition.

These, then, are the truly primitive molluscs, and in view of their unique position they have been removed from the Class Gastropoda altogether and put in a new class, the Monoplacophora. As if by way of confirmation, it has been found that certain early univalve shells show a thinning of the shell along a mid-line. A sequence of shells has been found which suggests that this led, by progressive erosion of the mid-line, from the univalve condition to the truly bivalved state. It only remains to find some link-forms connecting the Monoplacophora with the early cephalopods, and a reasonably tidy picture emerges, with the Archaetype vindicated and the Monoplacophora acting out its place in the fossil-record.

It therefore came as a surprise when someone fished up a living monoplacophoran off the coast of Mexico, in 1957. This find (Neopilina), is clearly a living creature; it has a limpet-type shell, a straight-through gut and no sign of twisting in its soft or hard parts. Further surprises occurred: initial investigations showed a curious repetition in some of its soft parts; for instance, it has five pairs of gills. This reduplication of organs is not unknown among the molluscs, but in view of the primitive positions of Neopilina it led to a provocative suggestion—could this multiple-organ feature be a reflection of the annelid/arthropodan state? Zoologists have long debated the origin of the Mollusca. It would be intriguing if a connection could be found in the fossil world which could truly link the Arthropoda with the Mollusca. But so far the oldest Cambrian strata contain fossils which show the two phyla to have been already quite distinct. It is often true, however, that the oldest fossils are not necessarily the most primitive, and a connection may yet be established.

Once the molluscs were created, there were six ways of life open to them; they could sit on the sea (or lake) floor, burrow under it, crawl over it, swim, drift, or struggle forth onto dry land.

CEPHALOPODS

The cephalopods mostly chose to swim, and stayed in the sea, and the remaining modes of life were taken up by the bivalves and gastropods. Perhaps it is misleading to use the expression 'chose to swim', but it can be said that the chambered, conical, air-filled shells of the cephalopods, whether straight or curled, are generally suited to the swimming mode of life. In most of the older groups the shell is external, and the animal is housed in the last chamber of the shell. If growth is incomplete, further growth entails the formation of additional dividing walls (septa), and the animal shifts forward so that it is always sited in the last chamber.

An important feature in these cephalopods is the existence of a hard-walled tube (siphuncle) which extends from the last chamber to the apex of the shell. It seems that this siphuncle accommodated a strand of living tissue which enabled the animal, amongst other things, to adjust the gas-pressure in its chambers. It so happens that only one genus of these old-style cephalopods survives—the famous *Nautilus* of the South-West Pacific. *Nautilus* has been observed to spend much of the day resting near to the sea-floor, but at night-time it swims, body downwards and shell upwards, in the traditional cephalopod fashion, with its buoyant shell keeping it in a position of stability. Contrary to early opinion, the *Nautilus* does not swim or drift on the surface of the water (see Fig. 17).

Although many of the older cephalopods favoured the *Nautilus* type of shell and way of life, some of them began a totally new approach to the matter. Carboniferous times saw the first belemnoids, and by Mesozoic times the bullet-shaped *internal* skeletons of these organisms frequent the sediments—sometimes so numerously that the sediment is often nothing more than a packed mass of belemnites. (Belemnite is the term commonly used for the bullet-shaped internal skeletons and Fig. 8 illustrates one of these.)

It is evident from considering the evolution of the belemnoids that they come from nautiloids (probably in mid-Palaeozoic times) which enveloped their own shells with the soft tissue of their bodies. A relic of the pre-envelopment stage lies in the tiny vestigial

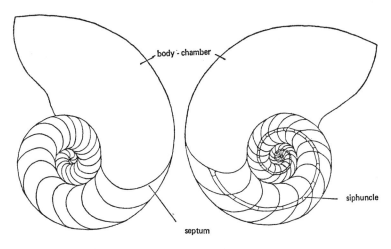

body - chamber

siphuncle

septum

Fig. 17   *Interior of Nautilus*

chambered skeleton within the open end of a well-preserved belemnite, and the internal nature of the belemnoid shell is recognizable
by the impressions of soft organs on the outside of the belemnite.
It is also clear from a study of present-day cephalopods that the
internal skeleton allows the creature far more speed and mobility
than the cumbersome external shell of *Nautilus*.

Certain squids leap out of the water like flying fish and sometimes rise to heights of over 12 ft before re-entering the sea. Many
squids hunt for prey like fish. The octopus, it is true, tends to be
sluggish and prefers waiting in a nest of its victims' bones and
shells for its prey to swim into the trap. But its speed, once it
moves into action, is quite remarkable. The octopus, incidently,
has taken the shell-reduction tendency of the cephalopods to an
extreme by abolishing it altogether. A further eccentricity displayed
by this type of cephalopod is seen in the octopus *Argonauta*, which,
though it has no true shell, is capable (if female) of manufacturing
a frail egg-case (the 'paper nautilus') which looks startlingly like
an ammonite, though in fact it is unchambered and is built by an
entirely different method from the ammonite's shell.

Other cephalopods include the nautiloids and ammonoids, the
former including the already-mentioned *Nautilus*. The ammonoids
are an extinct group, but during their period of existence (Devonian-
Cretaceous) provided the sediments of the sea with hosts of spiral

C

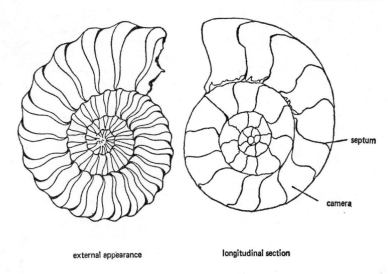

external appearance   longitudinal section

Fig. 18 *Ammonites*

shells ('ammonites') which, owing to their proliferation, ease of recognition, and the short time-span of each species' existence, make superb zoning fossils (see Fig. 18). That is to say, the age of the rock being investigated may be readily ascertained from any ammonites contained therein. Of course, some rocks contain no ammonites—perhaps they were non-marine, or the fossils have been leached away by percolating water, or there were no ammonoids in that part of the sea at the time that the sediment was formed—but on the whole, ammonoids having been the free-swimming creatures they were, fossils are both widespread and numerous. The discovery of an ammonite is an unrivalled experience. In addition to the glamour of being extinct, these shells exhibit a great structural beauty in the mathematical perfection of their spirally-curved shells.

Ammonites are frequently of great size, and specimens the size of cartwheels are not uncommon. The author, while on the Isle of Wight (England) with some companions, found preserved in iron-rich sandstone an ammonite weighing over 100 kg (220 lb), and measuring 45 cm (1 ft 6 in) across. The struggle to raise the fossil to the top of the cliff from which it had originally fallen was no less great than the achievement of persuading the ferry officials that such an object could be described as 'hand-luggage' (and therefore cheap to convey) rather than 'freight' (and therefore requiring an expensive supplementary ticket). This fossil was, however, tiny compared with some of the Cretaceous species of *Pachydiscus*, $2\frac{1}{2}$ m (i.e. $8\frac{1}{2}$ ft) in diameter.

Some of the Triassic and Cretaceous ammonites present a curiously coiled appearance. These are the heteromorphs (i.e., different shapes), and they seem to be ill-adapted to swimming. Comparative studies in a tank of water, using model shells with weights where the body belonged, suggest that these creatures were more adapted to crawling on or near the sea-floor, like gastropods; or perhaps floating like jellyfish, in accordance with the weight/buoyancy ratio. For some unknown reason these heteromorphs are not known from Jurassic rocks (see Fig. 19).

Fig. 19   *Inferred living positions of certain Cephalopods*

BIVALVES

The bivalves (Latin for 'two-doors') are sub-aquatic bottom-dwellers, generally breathing water in and filtering microscopic food particles out of it with their gills, and then exhaling the waste water. Though bivalves are wholly aquatic, they are by no means wholly marine. The shape of the shell is far from conservative, and varies greatly in appearance, and though it is sometimes subjected to an evolutional trend towards shell-reduction, it is never lost altogether as in the cephalopods (octopus) or gastropods (slugs). Three principal modes of life are open to the bivalves (Fig. 9 and the accompanying text explain this).

The adaptability of the bivalve shell is very clearly seen in *Tridacna*, the giant clam. Here the normal, hinge-uppermost type of existence has been abandoned, since, unlike most bivalves, *Tridacna* has added to the gill-feeding habit by employing symbiotic algae in the greatly-developed tissues in the upper part of the body; the algae synthesize carbohydrates, which the giant clam can use as food. It is thus advantageous for *Tridacna* to open its shells towards the sunlight, but instead of adopting an upside-down position, the soft parts of the body have stayed constant while the shell has moved through 180° to open upwards. This great mobility of the shell with respect to the soft parts, is remarkable. There are stories of divers having their feet caught in the shells of giant clams, and being held there till they drown or the clam, continually agitated by the presence of a foreign body, severs the leg by its closing power. To quote Darwin: 'We stayed a long time in the lagoon (of Keeling Id.), examining the fields of coral and the gigantic clam-shells, into which if a man were to put his hand, he would not, as long as the animal lived, be able to withdraw it.'

Pecten, familiar in the form of ashtrays and as a symbol for the Shell Oil Company (one of its co-founders was a shell-collector, hence its name and mascot), is a rare example of a bivalve which can swim. If scared by a starfish or similar enemy, *Pecten* can snap its valves together and 'swim' a short distance to escape, though it normally prefers to lie quietly on the sea-floor on its larger valve. *Pecten* and *Lima* are noteworthy for their many steely-blue 'eyes' (simple light-sensitive organs). *Brechites* is a bizarre type of bivalve which has its valves embedded to its burrow in a calcareous lining. A species of *Ephippodonta* has its valves perpetually in the 180° open position, and enveloped by the tissues of its body, since it lives inside the burrow of an Australian shrimp, and flattened to the burrow wall to be out of the way.

Fossil bivalves have long been studied for their attractive appearance, but have latterly acquired additional importance because of the ability to tell the palaeontologist how the creatures lived and what the conditions of deposition were like. With certain exceptions, they make indifferent zoning fossils. Sometimes they occur as fossilized shell-banks or shell-beds. In Dorset, England, there is an 'oyster bed' up to 10 ft thick and which can be traced over 20 miles. It is virtually a solid mass of fossil oysters, and beds of this type are common throughout the world.

GASTROPODS

The gastropods, familiar in many parts of the world as garden snails, are, in numbers of species, more numerous than the bivalves and cephalopods, though it may come as a surprise that there are more snails in the sea than on the land. They did not become really numerous till the Cenozoic Era, and seldom form massive shell-beds as the bivalves do, but in many Cenozoic formations they exhibit an astonishing variety of species. Like the bivalves, gastropods sometimes occur in fresh-water deposits, but unlike the bivalves they are also to be found in purely terrestrial formations, along with the reptiles, mammals, and other dwellers of the land-surface.

The transition from water to land is a study in itself, and merits a brief mention here. The gastropods, like most animals, originated in the sea; the constant temperature, plentiful food, and omnipresent water are three vital factors in maintaining primitive life. The gastropod gill, however, can adapt itself breathing fresh water or air (in the latter case becoming a sort of 'lung'). Curiously enough, while many gastropod groups are marine and have end-members in the fresh-water habitats, the transition to air-breathing does not necessarily have to take place from fresh water, and is sometimes achieved directly by migration from the sea. The winkles include gastropods which, living normally in the sea, can tolerate long hours exposed to the air and sun at low tide. It is but a short step from the winkle stage to the purely terrestrial stage. *Ampullarius* is a gastropod which is truly amphibious in that it can breathe air or water equally well. Some of the land gastropods have taken their adaptations to extremes, and favour desert environments in which only camels and men can survive. A species of *Helix* can live in the Algerian desert, where temperatures reach to 43° C (110° F). *Bithynia*, on the other hand, lives in hot springs in the Pyrenees, while *Limnaea peregra var. geysericola* prefers the geyser-water of Iceland.

Contrary to what one might think, rivers and lakes offer few barriers to fresh-water or terrestrial gastropods. Floodings enable the former types to spread rapidly over a continent, while drifting vegetation or droughts encourage the latter to do the same. *Helix aspersa*, the common garden snail, is world-wide in occurrence, though introduced by man outside Europe. Another piece of gastropod perversity is provided by the operculum, the lid-like piece of shell embedded in the hind part of the gastropod's body, which closes over the aperture like a little door when the animal has retreated into its shell. Whereas one might expect the operculum to be characteristic of land-gastropods, which have to hibernate or aestivate for long periods and to put up with extremes of all sorts of environmental conditions, it is seldom to be found in the often terrestrial subclass of the Pulmonata (lung-bearing gastropods). It is a characteristic example of other gastropod subclasses, many or most of whose members are marine; even when the operculum *is* present, it often does not fit the aperture exactly. Some Pulmonata do, however, secrete a tough, membranous skin or 'epiphragm' which serves the same purpose as the operculum. The island of Jamaica is remarkable for being one of the few places where the number of operculate terrestrial gastropods exceeds the number of Pulmonata.

The study of the Gastropoda has long been enhanced by the natural beauty of their helical shells, but in recent decades there has been a tendency for research into this group to lag somewhat. Discouragement seems to arise from their comparative lack of stratigraphic value (that is, they are seldom useful for estimating the age of a rock), and the embarrassing abundance of species which make an overall knowledge of the class, or even part of it, very difficult to acquire.

MISCELLANEOUS OTHER MARINE FOSSILS

The heading for this section is, perhaps, rather optimistic, since it would take many pages of this book merely to list the 'miscellaneous marine fossils', let alone describe them. However, from this wealth of palaeontological material it is possible to choose a few items of quaint or curious significance.

Insect fossils are rare in marine rocks, since the tracheal system of respiration of the insects, so successful in the aerial environment, is less effective when immersed in water. The diving beetles, for instance, have to carry the air with them and drown if they do not return to the surface, whale-like, to renew their supply occasionally. However, there are many arthropod groups other than the insects which do occur in marine rocks; trilobites are a famous extinct group, being limited to the Palaeozoic Era while crabs and lobsters are scarce in rocks older than the Mesozoic. The tiny but abundant ostracods range from the Palaeozoic to the present day.

The ostracods are instructive in that they exemplify not only a group of fossils eminently useful to the palaeontologist, but also the difficulties of communication between the palaeontologist and his colleague in the Zoology department. Ostracods are small, usually a millimetre or so long, shrimp-like creatures with bivalved shells which look remarkably like miniaturized bivalved molluscs. In favourable conditions, they swarm in immense numbers, being almost entirely an aquatic group and mainly concerned with moving in or over the sea or lake bottom in search of food. When they die their shells are buried by the million in the sediment, and they thus become microfossils, in the sense that a microscope is needed to study them properly, though the naked eye may detect the larger ones. The advantages of the ostracods to the palaeontologist are threefold:

(a) being frequently numerous, they are easy to find, and can be studied on a statistical basis

(b) they are often good indicators of the environment in which they lived and died

(c) they may also prove useful for estimating the age of the rock containing them.

In fact, the term 'ostracodologist' has arisen to describe the specialist in this field. However, the fact that the shell of the ostracod readily fossilizes, but the soft parts do not, is a point of difficulty regarding the study of this group, since zoologists prefer to classify them according to their soft parts while palaeontologists have to restrict their attention to the hard parts. A clearly-understood classification is essential to all palaeontological work, and when one worker is deducing a likely environment for a certain type of ostracod which is closely related to a certain living ostracod, it is preferable for the authority on the living ostracods to have the same concept of classification as the authority on the fossils, otherwise they may find themselves in animated agreement on two creatures which are quite different. Attention has been directed to this problem, however, and the difficulties are being tackled.

The Foraminifera (familiarly called 'forams') are another group of microfossils which share the ostracods' virtues, and they have been studied even more intensively because of their great usefulness

in unravelling the problems of oil geology. For many years now
these minute, one-celled creatures with astonishingly complicated
skeletons (occasionally large enough to be visible to the naked eye)
have been the focus of intensive research actuated by all the power
and riches of the oil companies. The forams are mostly marine or
brackish-water creatures, and many of them live on the sea-floor,
but certain of them have, particularly in the Cretaceous and later
periods, taken up a planktonic mode of life, resulting in the formation in the deep sea of foraminiferal oozes, a mud composed of
the skeletons of countless millions of forams, which may later
undergo compaction to form a chalk, marl or limestone. The Chalk
of North-West Europe, famous for the white cliffs of Dover and the

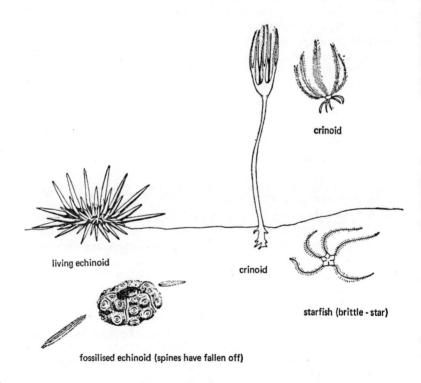

crinoid

living echinoid

crinoid

starfish (brittle - star)

fossilised echinoid (spines have fallen off)

Fig. 20   *Echinoderms*

Champagne vineyards, is a Cretaceous accumulation of compacted ooze rich in forams. Forams are sensitive to temperature and can be used as temperature- or depth-indicators (deeper water is colder as a rule), the latter usage being very important in deciding the geography of ancient seas, reefs and coastlines which may contain or be the source of oil.

The echinoderms form a large and important group of fossils—starfish (stelleroids), sea-urchins (echinoids) and sea-lilies (crinoids) are all represented in the fossil record—see Fig. 20—the last two more plentifully than the first. Starfish are noteworthy for their predatory way of life; they are the enemy of most small bivalves, whose muscles are severely taxed by the starfish's ability to pull with its arms for long periods of time. Echinoids are spiny little creatures whose barbaric attitude to swimmers' feet is all too well-known in warmer waters while crinoids are peaceful, plant-like creatures often spending their lives rooted to the same spot on the sea-floor. The unique properties of the echinoderms single them out strongly as a separate phylum in the animal world. They have a five-rayed symmetry (we, like most active animals, have a bilateral symmetry—two arms, two legs, and so forth); a skeleton composed of plates, each comprised of a single crystal of calcite; a purely marine habitat; and so on.

It is noteworthy, however, that some of the purely Palaeozoic echinoderms are less strongly characterized, and indeed the proliferation of radical (and often abortive) new stocks at that time has yielded some palaeontological surprises. For instance, the Calcichordata—see p. 54—has been created to include echinoderm-like fossils of Palaeozoic age which bear, on closer examination, the impress of soft parts on their skeletons which, according to recent interpretation, represent soft parts of the type exhibited today by the Chordata (vertebrates and related creatures). Yet the general appearance of these fossils is of the echinoderm type. Are the Calcichordata, then, the link between our own phylum, the Chordata, and the Echinodermata? It would seem plausible. Fig. 14 shows a few of the Calcichordata recently described in the light of modern views. They may look rather different from the fish, but then there are plenty of worm-like creatures alive today exhibiting sufficient anatomical similarities to the vertebrates to warrant their inclusion in the Phylum Chordata, while in their general appearance they are no more than just 'worms' to the average fisherman.

At the other end of the scale, and as far from the structural complexity of the Chordata as one can be without actually descending into the realm of one-celled creatures, is the Phylum

Porifera (sponges). Most of these are marine; the common bath-sponge (nowadays widely replaced by a rubber or artificial substitute), is a sponge of the non-fossilizable type, but many sponges contain a hard, gritty mass of tiny spikes ('spicules') of calcite or silica in their tissues, and some types even have these spicules united into a rigid skeleton, though this does not have the same predictable regularity of shape as our skeletons. Sponges tend to be small and modest in cold latitudes like Britain's, but can be magnificent, brightly-coloured, vase-like objects, and, though world-wide, are commoner in the warm, shelf waters. Their value to palaeontology is small, but they often have indirect effects. Thus the occurrence of flints (silica nodules which fracture in glass-like curves) and cherts (silica which fractures in hackly, jagged lines) can often be related to an abundance of sponges with silica spicules in the sea when the rock was laid down. The spicules, being tiny, are readily dissolved (just as granular sugar dissolves quicker than lump or big-crystal sugar) and re-precipitated as the flint (or chert) nodules.

Brachiopods (see Fig. 21) are often dismissed by biologists as a 'minor group', but as far as palaeontology is concerned they were quite the reverse in the past. Throughout the Palaeozoic and to some extent the Mesozoic rocks, these bivalved shells abound. However, they are bivalved in appearance only, since their true

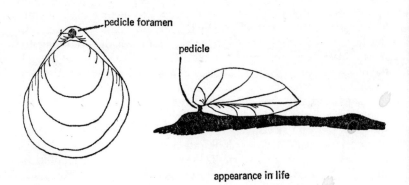

Fig. 21   *Brachiopods*

nature, both zoological and palaeontological, is utterly different from the molluscan Bivalvia. Zoological distinctions are hardly likely to impress the fossil collector, but he should note the characteristic 'pedicle foramen' (see Fig. 21), which is a hole in the end of one of the valves designed to accomodate the living, muscular pedicle, which anchors the brachiopod to the sea-floor in a manner similar to the already-described non-living tuft of hair-like byssus of certain Bivalvia. Not all Brachiopoda have this pedicle foramen— the animal world is constantly eluding exact definition.

THE CORALS, AND THEIR INFORMATION ON THE SLOWING-DOWN OF THE EARTH

Mention has already been made of the nature and history of the great ocean reefs, and the part that the corals have to play in them. Further remarks to complete a summary of this group must include both a mention of the solitary corals and the information provided by the study of the corals' growth-lines.

Solitary corals are far more widespread than reef corals. Whereas the lattter are restricted to warm, shallow tropical sea-water (see p. 58), the former can occur in most temperatures, depths and latitudes. Growths of living corals throng parts of the sea-floor off the Norwegian coast up to 69° N, and corals have been dredged from the abyss where eternal darkness prevails. Most modern corals require a firm base for their weighty little skeletons, and tend to avoid muddy sea-floors. However, certain corals have adopted ingenious methods of survival on a muddy bottom. *Calceola*, of the Middle Devonian period, has a slipper-like appearance (Latin calceolus: a small shoe or slipper), so that it can rest horizontally on the soft sea-floor.

A glance at almost any bivalve or gastropod will reveal that the exterior of the shell is marked by numerous concentric growth-lines, these lines always curving round the spot which represents the youthful shell. If the animal has been severely attacked or been through a period of famine, or any other time of reduced capacity to build its shell, the growth-lines bunch closely together. On the other hand, widely spaced growth-lines denote livelier shell-building —and there are other factors also at work.

It is to some extent possible, therefore, to reconstruct the molluscs's record of its fluctuating environment from the growth-lines. This has also been looked into with the corals, since they too have growth-lines on their epitheca (outermost shell), and the individual coral's history can be traced in the record of the epitheca.

A coral normally feeds off the plankton, and there is evidence that at least some of this plankton's movements in the ocean are related to the phases of the moon : presumably the moon's light is operative here. Daily, monthly, and yearly cycles are visible in the epithecal growth-lines, and a study of these gives a clue to the age of the coral. Most intriguing of all, this principle has been extended to fossil corals, and it is found, for instance, that Devonian corals tend to indicate yearly cycles of 400 days instead of 365. This means that the day had, in those times, 22 hours. In other words, the earth has been slowing down like a top which is slowed down principally by the braking effect of the air's friction. The earth must similarly be slowed down by the friction of the tides flowing to and fro round the coastlines of the world.

5   The First Non-Marine Life

*'And the desert shall rejoice, and blossom as the rose' – Isaiah
35:1*

DEVONIAN PLANTS

A remarkably clear picture of the Middle Devonian terrestrial life
has been gained by the fortuitous occurrence of silicified peat at
Rhynie, in Scotland. This Rhynie chert not only contains a number
of plants which are clearly but a short step from their ancestral
seaweeds, but also an arthropod fauna including the oldest known
insects. The plants are mostly slender, erect stems which spread
across the land by 'runners' (horizontal stems). The presence of
moisture-regulating pores (stomata) in the Rhynie plants qualifies
them for classification as land plants, and though they were of
lowly size they seem to have been fairly numerous at Rhynie. The
preservation is by a kind of silica impregnation, probably due to
the charging of the local bog-water with silica from the volcanic
activity nearby, and preservation is so perfect that thin sections
reveal cell nuclei and the presence of fungi. A curious footnote
may be added to this paragraph with reference to the *Psilotum*, a
simple land-plant, still to be found alive today and resembling,
though perhaps not related to, the Devonian Rhynie plants.

The Devonian was a time of great advancement in the fossil
plants. For one thing, new types of plant emerged. It is not pro-
prosed to describe these here except to note that seed-formation
had not yet begun to be clearly developed, and plants with woody
stems of tree-like dimensions had begun to appear. The foliage was
mainly of the fern type, and the appearance of coaly seams, in
Russia and elsewhere, indicates that the vegetation cover of the
land-surface was well advanced by the end of the Devonian. The
invertebrate groups reveal no distinctive change in their Devonian
distribution, but the vertebrates show a marked advance in the
latter part of the period. The fish of the rivers and lakes of the

earlier Devonian fresh-water stages begun not only to invade the land as amphibians, but also to spread into the sea.

FISH CLASSIFICATION

Class Agnatha (armoured, jawless)
Class Placodermi (armoured, with jaws)
  Order Arthrodira
  Order Antiarchi
  (other orders)
Class Chondrichthyes (sharks, rays)
Class Osteichthyes (bony fish : very common nowadays)
  Subclass Acanthodii
  Subclass Actinopterygii (ray-fins)
  Subclass Sarcopterygii
    Order Dipnoi (lungfish)
    Order Crossopterygii (lobe-fins)
      Suborder Coelocanthini (includes *Latimeria*)
      Suborder Rhipidistia (ancestral to the land-vertebrates)

DEVONIAN FISH : THEIR ORIGINS

The earliest known fish-remains are fragments of armour in Ordovician rocks which also contain evidence of deposition near a shoreline. However, it is none too easy to be sure whether these early fish were truly marine or whether they were non-marine and their remains were swept into the sea by currents. The existence today in the sea of living primitive organisms related to, but less complex than, the vertebrates (acorn worms, sea squirts, etc.) suggests rather vaguely that the former is true.

THE AGNATHA

The most primitive, though not the earliest well-documented fish is *Jamoytius kerwoodi* (Upper Silurian of Scotland). This has no external armour, and what skeleton it has seems to have been cartilaginous, and therefore its preservation is very fortunate. It shows some very primitive properties of construction which strongly suggest that it is related to the humble, boneless invertebrate chordates such as *Amphioxus*, which is alive today in our seas. Other Agnatha have external armour (see Fig. 22).

Two curious features of these earliest fish may be mentioned. In the first place, they are jawless, having nothing more complicated

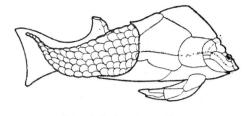

Pterichthyodes (Class Placodermi)

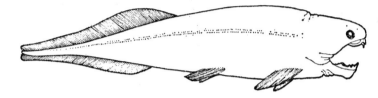

Dinichthys (Class Placodermi)

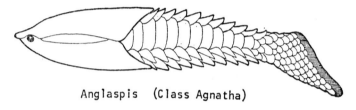

Anglaspis (Class Agnatha)

Fig. 22 *Primitive fish*

than hole-like mouths with which to feed; and secondly they are armoured with bony scales and plates. The first condition gives rise to the name of this group (Agnatha), and implies that the creatures may have been mud-eaters; the second condition is the main reason why these fish are found at all as fossils, since their internal bones were not as a rule preserved and presumably were largely composed of cartilage which, though tough enough to form a skeleton (the skeletons of sharks and rays are formed of this material), contain no mineral salts and so will not fossilize. These fish were usually covered with a coat of scales and armour plates, the latter covering the head area.

The Agnatha extend from the Ordovician to Devonian times, with some specialized modern representatives which, having no armour, have no fossil record. The early Agnatha seem to have been non-marine in their habitat, and all the variety of Devonian fish (to be described below) and consequent land-vertebrates, were descended from them. The modern Agnatha have achieved fame in an unexpected quarter by causing the death of King Henry I of England (d. 1135), who is reputed to have died of a 'surfeit of lampreys'.

The question arises: how did the bony armour of these fish originate? Mention has already been made of the Calcichordata (see p. 54), with their calcium carbonate skeletons, and their resemblance to the vertebrates. The possibility of the origin of bone as a calcium/phosphorus store is mentioned below; at any rate, there were predators from the invertebrate world both in the sea and in fresh water which may have made armour-plating necessary for these early vertebrates. The eurypterids, fresh-water arthropods of large size (up to 9 ft long) with the appearance of scorpions, and far from jawless, must have been formidable competitors.

As far as the sea was concerned, any Devonian fish were in direct competition with the cephalopods which, if they were anything like their present-day descendants, were carnivorous and armed with prehensile tentacles. The fish seem to have survived the rigours of the times well, though with varying fortunes.

THE PLACODERMS

By Lower Devonian times the Agnatha had begun to give rise to a new group of fish, the placoderms. These had solid armour-plating like some of the Agnatha (Greek placos: flat+dermos: skin), but the vital difference between these creatures and the Agnatha was the possession of jaws by the placoderms. These jaws seem to have originated in the pressing into service, as eating devices, of the front bones of the gill-arch-system of the Agnatha. In so doing the granularity of the armour-surface developed into teeth in the region of the jaws. Indeed, the distinction betwen the exoskeleton (armour) and the endoskeleton (bones) of them and their descendants is reflected in our own bodies, where the teeth are the exoskeleton, or what remains of it, and our bones are the endoskeleton. In fact, the dentine of our teeth can be seen at the other end of the palaeontological story in the agnathan armour.

Thus, armed with jaws, the placoderms multiplied and diversified in the fresh waters of the Devonian land. Two major groups appeared; the arthrodires and antiarchs. The arthrodires had a massively armoured head and 'shoulders', and some very strange jaw-structures. In our jaws, as in most vertebrates, the teeth are fixed onto jaw-bones, but in the arthrodires the 'teeth' are mere projections of the jaw-bones, generally in the form of incisor-like tusks before, and scissor-like shearing edges behind. These fish, which showed a drift towards marine life in later Devonian times, attained large dimensions in some species—*Dinichthys* reached a length of 30 ft (10 metres)—and, to judge from the powerful jaws, must have proved formidable competition for other kinds of fish. The antiarchs, on the other hand, were characterized by small mouths and a flattened underside which both suggest a bottom-dwelling existence, like many bottom-dwelling fish today of a similarly flattened appearance.

THE SHARKS AND RAYS

From the placoderms presumably arose the two great fish divisions which, in contrast to the placoderms and their agnathan ancestors, are still very much alive today. These are the cartilaginous fish (sharks and rays) and the bony fish, the latter forming the majority of the fish complement of our seas and rivers. The shark group, as one might expect from the preceding remarks on the subject of cartilage, does not provide a very detailed fossil record. However, it can be said that the group is almost entirely marine, apparently from as far back as its mid-Devonian origins. It would appear that the calcification of the internal skeleton of the placoderms, which is often incomplete, was arrested or put into reverse with the emergence of the sharks, and although it is true that the beautifully-preserved sharks' teeth to be found in many rocks are the beginner's usual introduction to the world of fossil fish, one rarely finds more than a tooth, and this is the only part likely to show where a shark once fell to the sea-floor.

THE BONY FISH

With the bony fish, however, the situation is quite different. We naturally have a good record of their history because the internal skeleton is more or less completely preservable. It would appear that the early history of the bony fish was in fresh water, and the marine habitat was reached in the late Palaeozoic Era. From the first, two principal types of bony fish are evident: the Actinopterygii and Sarcopterygii—the former being today amazingly diversified and numerous, and some like the sea-horse and stone-fish, look hardly like fish at all. A third and relatively minor group, the Acanthodii, distinguished by their bony spines which formed the cutwater edges of their fins, are limited to the Palaeozoic Era.

SARCOPTERYGII

The lung-fish and the coelocanth, however, are much more important from the evolutionary point of view, since it is from creatures
of their type that the land vertebrates arose. The lung-fish, of
which three types are known alive today, lives in inland tropical
lakes, and when these dry up in the dry season, some lung-fish
bury themselves in the mud and, half-asleep, breathe air with their
lungs. This possession of a lung by a fish may seem surprising, but
in fact many fish of the ray-fin group have an air sac (to provide
the fish with a variable buoyancy organ), and the lung-fish's lung
is no doubt homologous with this. Indeed, as far back as the
antiarchs air-sacs have been found, and for that matter the gastropods have also demonstrated their ability to breathe air instead of
water (see p. 69). It is in the coelocanth *Latimeria* that we find the
closest modern relative of the fish-amphibian transition of the
Palaeozoic Era.

The coelocanths are a group of sarcopterygians which were
thought to have died out in the Cretaceous period until one,
Latimeria, was fished alive from a mere 240 ft depth off the coast
of South Africa in 1938. The characteristic feature of this type of
fish is that it is lobe-finned rather than ray-finned (see Fig. 23). That
is, a fleshy lobe containing muscles and bones connects the fin
with the body, and the fin is thus operated by this lobe, whereas
in the ray-finned group the fin is mostly a device of skin supported
by ray-like bones, with only a small lobe (if any) supporting it.

Fig. 23   *The Coelocanth (Latimeria)*

Although both types of bony fish, and, for that matter, some of the placoderms themselves, may have had an equal chance of survival in dried-up pools in the Upper Devonian landscape by breathing air via their air-sacs, the lobe-fin types (Crossopterygii) had a distinct advantage in that they could wriggle on their muscular fins from one dried-up pool to the next, thus allowing them to find water while their rivals were dying in any unusually long drought. Thus developed the first amphibians, some time in the late Devonian period, perhaps more as a consequence of the fish struggling *back* to the water than out of it.

It was not the coelocanths themselves, but the rhipidistians, a closely related group, which evidently achieved this momentous step onto dry land, and while it is true that a ray-fin fish, the mud-skipper, can be seen today crawling over mangrove roots and breathing in air and using its ray-fins as legs (though it has to return to water periodically, like a whale in reverse, to obtain water for its gills), the niche has already been filled by the Amphibia. *Latimeria*, the 'living-fossil' is of interest in that its lobe-fins present us with the living evidence of the construction of the first amphibians' limbs.

THE ORIGIN OF BONE AND TEETH

Before continuing with the history of the early land-vertebrates, some speculations as to the origin of bones and teeth must be mentioned. Although the origin of bone is by no means understood with any certainty, it has been suggested that its initial purpose was to act as a calcium- and phosphorus-store, bones being a mixture of organic materials with calcium phosphate. Calcium is necessary for growth and muscular action; moreover it must be kept at the correct concentration, since too much calcium may cause illness or death. Phosphorus is vital in the production of proteins and other bio-chemical processes. A fish must take in phosphorus salts for its needs, and it must also cope with an environment which may be at times very deficient in calcium and phosphorus, especially in fresh water. Bone is thus a convenient store for these elements. It is noteworthy that the early armoured fish possessed a type of bone similar to the material of our teeth, which is a compact, non-cellular calcium phosphate material and, owing to the lack of living organic cells therein, is difficult to introduce into solution in the bloodstream. Hence the phosphorus-calcium store was effectively increased in the true bone of the more advanced verte-brates, where the living cellular structure enabled the calcium and phosphorus to be readily exchanged to and from the bloodstream. The reader may care to reflect, next time he or she suffers from toothache, that there is no clear physiological reason why our teeth should be sensitive to pain. It seems likely that the reason for the nerve-bearing tubules in the dentine is that they are a relic of the tubule-ridden exoskeleton of the Palaeozoic armoured fish from which they are derived, the purpose of which was to retain tactile sensitivity through the otherwise non-living armour.

Once the Carboniferous Period had dawned, the hectic phase of vertebrate evolution began to slow down. The amphibians, which had first begun to appear in the late Devonian, rapidly became well-established, some of them retaining to this day the sinuous body-movement in their walking gait that denotes their fish ancestry. The primitive amphibian skull is but a short step from the crosso-pterygian fish's skull. Of course the amphibians are still not entirely free from the water, but their derivatives, the reptiles (first to be seen in the Carboniferous rocks), solved this problem by encasing their eggs in shells, as the birds do. As far as the fish were con-cerned, the miscellaneous groups of the placoderms had mostly died out by Carboniferous times, and the waters were populated mainly by bony fish and (in the sea) sharks and such like.

A SUMMARY OF THE DEVONIAN LIFE

In reviewing the Devonian, it would appear that there was no land vertebrate life in evidence till the end of the period, though fish life was vigorous and underwent much diversification. Invertebrate non-marine life was rather scanty on the land, but in the water, bivalves and gastropods appeared, presumably migrants from the sea; and large bivalves, like *Amnigenia*, look rather like modern fresh-water shells such as *Anodonta*. The eurypterids, with their evil-looking claws, inhabited many of the rivers, and the effects of drought can be seen in various fish-beds where dozens of well-preserved archaic fish have been fossilized where they had died, close-packed in the bottom of their dried-up pools. The earth, beautified by the appearance of trees which were forerunners of the great coal forests of the Carboniferous, rotated, it would seem, once every 22 hours.

THE CARBONIFEROUS PERIOD

The Carboniferous rocks of the world provide one of the most fascinating contrasts in the study of historical geology, namely, the

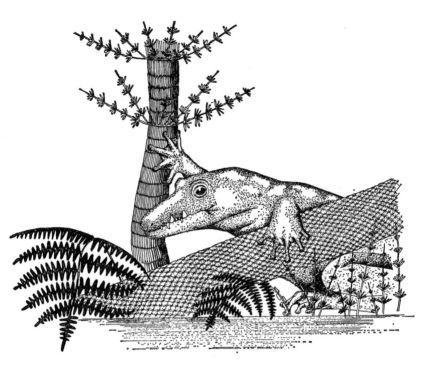

Fig. 24 *An Amphibian in a Carboniferous coal-forest*

co-existence of dense forests of Amazonian dimensions in the northern hemisphere, fringed by seas rich in marine life, while in the southern hemisphere a glacial age spread its ice over an area comparable with, or perhaps greater than, present-day Antarctica, scratching the rocks and strewing boulders around as ice always does.

THE COAL FORESTS

Leaving aside, for the moment, the explanation for this paradox, a review of the life of the Carboniferous period may be made. By Upper Carboniferous times, when many of the rich coal-bearing strata of the northern hemisphere were being formed, the flora had advanced both in size and variety. A typical Carboniferous coal-forest (see Fig. 24) might be expected to have gymnosperms, lycopods, pteridosperms, ferns and Equisetales (horsetails) in abundance:

Gymnosperms: (Greek gymnos: naked; sperma: seed) plants wherein the seed is situated nakedly on a modified leaf, represented today by the conifers (pine, fir, larch, etc.).

Lycopods: (Greek lycos: wolf; pous: foot) plants where the leaves are usually fixed onto the stem in a spirally-arranged fashion, represented today by *Lycopodium*, a small herbaceous plant.

Pteridosperms: (Greek pteris: fern; sperma: seed) plants now extinct with fern-like foliage and yet having seeds.

Ferns: plants with characteristically indented foliage and having spores rather than seeds (N.B.: seed is a reproduction device, the product of fertilization, enveloped by a membrane and often provided with a food-store: spores are reproduction devices with no store).

Equisetales: (Latin equus: horse; seta: bristle) plants with leaves which occur in whorls along the stem, represented today by 'horsetails'.

No doubt other types of plant thrived—algae in the ponds, lichens on boughs, fungi on rotten wood, liverworts by springs and streams, mosses, etc.—but these soft plants left little or no fossil record. The most striking thing about the coal-forest plants is their size: 100 ft (30 m) was not an uncommon height for a Carboniferous tree, a dimension especially impressive when one compares these plants with their modern descendants which, with the exception of the gymnosperms, are small, weak objects. It is the death and compression of these forests which provides the world with much of its coal, and the presence of roots in the rock below the coal indicates that the coal has formed more or less in situ—i.e., it has formed where the trees responsible for it grew.

It is also possible not only to enumerate the types of plant present in these forests, but also to reconstruct a picture of their inter-relationships. For instance, in a study of many thousands of plant fossils from the South Wales coalfield it has been concluded that, whereas *Calamites* (an equisetalean) and *Cordaites* (a gymnosperm) were more or less uniformly distributed throughout the succession of rocks under investigation, the lower, wetter land was populated largely by lycopods, with pteridosperms and ferns living on the higher and dried ground. Coal itself can be classified into various types, bituminous coal being one derived directly from the coal forests, while boghead coal (a less commonly occurring variety, burning with an oily flame) is a type due to the accumulation of spores, algae, seeds, ets., in open pools.

Occasionally large, hard calcareous nodules are to be found in the coal. These 'coal balls' may be rich in excellently-preserved but fragmental plant material. From the observation that, in some examples at least, crystals of mineral salts within the cells have not deformed the cell-walls, it has been deduced that the plant material was infilled with minerals while it was still upright in the forest. In fact, the plants seem to have grown around a mineral-rich spring, become slowly petrified with salts in their tissues, died, and fell brittly in the spring there to be preserved as fragments in a matrix of calcite and other minerals—the coal-ball. The plants of the coal forest demonstrate by their size that the climate was congenial to plant growth and the frequent association of non-marine aquatic bivalves with the coal seams indicates that waterways were often nearby.

CONTINENTAL DRIFT

By no means all the earth was covered by coal forests in the Carboniferous Period. Apart from the oceanic areas, there are 'red beds' where desert-like conditions prevailed (in some countries they follow on from the coal measures), and other environments are in evidence. In the southern continents, the flora is, in contrast to the rich northern forests, represented by plants of which *Glossopteris* (a seed-bearing plant of debatable affinities) is the most characteristic. This occurrence of *Glossopteris* and its allies in South America, Australia, Antarctica, South Africa, and India, but rarely in the northern continents, gives strong confirmation to the theory of continental drift, along with the evidence of Upper Palaeozoic ice in the continents (see Fig. 25).

Close investigation of this Upper Palaeozoic ice evidence reveals that the scratchings on the subjacent rocks indicate an origin for the ice in regions which are now ocean, unless one fits the southern continents together as in a jigsaw. That is to say, the Upper Palaeozoic rock-scratchings in the Southern Hemisphere continents indicate that ice-sheets have travelled in various directions, some of which apparently call for the ice flowing from what is now open ocean. Since ice flows downhill, this is scarcely credible unless one allows for a pre-drift geographical situation in the Upper Palaeozoic, as shown in Fig. 25. Furthermore, the present distribution of the evidence for the Upper Palaeozoic ice-caps is so widely scattered that, wherever one chooses to postulate the position of

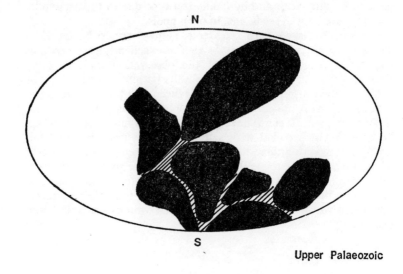

Upper Palaeozoic

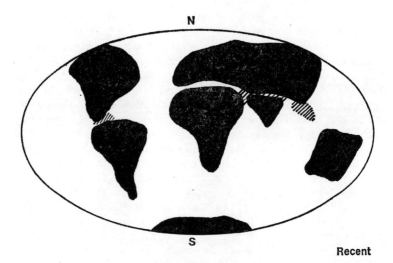

Recent

Fig. 25   *Continental drift*
Black areas are stable blocks. Shaded areas are additional
temporary land areas

the South Pole for that time, it is impossible to have all the ice-caps near enough to it to account for the existence of the ice, unless one allows for the breaking-up of the area by continental drift since the Upper Palaeozoic era. Once these continents are thus divorced from the northern continents and fitted together, the ice-caps can be united as a more or less single ice-sheet, forming in South America in the Lower Carboniferous period, spreading over Antarctica, South Africa and India in the Carboniferous, and withdrawing to Australia in the Permian, the ice being fringed by cool lands sometimes supporting the *Glossopteris* flora.

This super-continent has been called Gondwanaland, and it is tempting to ascribe the spread of the ice across it, to the drift of Gondwanaland across the South Pole in Upper Palaeozoic times, with the present appearance of the southern hemisphere being due to the Mesozoic break-up of Gondwanaland. This is the theory of continental drift, much favoured southern geologists and rather more cautiously favoured by northern geologists (in the U.S.S.R., in fact, Professor Beloussov adamantly insists that it is a figment of scientific imagination).

The northern continents, which may at that time have been a single unit ('Laurasia'), probably lay nearer the equator in Carboniferous times, and this could account for the coal-forests. Many people may find continental drift difficult to accept owing to their conviction that the sea-floor, under the oozes, is solid rock, but the difficulty here may be modified by the consideration that even the hardest rocks may be constrained to flow when the great forces of the earth's interior are at work over the immensity of geological time. The seemingly hard glacier will flow downhill over a period of hundreds of years, likewise the seemingly hard crust of the earth will flow just as readily over periods of millions of years. Many a fold in the hard strata exposed in cuttings and cliffs will demonstrate this fact. The only final proof of continental drift would appear to lie in its direct measurement, and a possible means of doing this may arise from a survey, by modern methods, from continent to continent, and to the moon. One of the fastest continental drifts (which may have slowed down, now, however) seems to have been the recession of India from Antarctica since the Carboniferous Period; a distance of 4,000 miles in c. 270,000,000 years, averaging approximately 2·5 cm per annum, which may be a measurable velocity.

CARBONIFEROUS ANIMALS

There being no birds, the coal forests must have been curiously silent compared with present-day forests. Primitive dragonflies with a 1 ft 10 in wingspan flew in the air, while cockroaches crawled below. Among other Carboniferous non-marine creatures, not necessarily inhabitants of the coal forests, were the vertebrates (amphibians, reptiles and fish). These included amphibians up to 15 ft long (*Eogyrinus*), and there is no lack of number or variety shown by this group. But the reptile fossils are relatively scanty, and limited to the later part of the Carboniferous. The non-marine fish were mainly bony fish (collectively termed the 'palaeoniscoids'), while the sea was inhabited by the cartilaginous fish (sharks and their allies).

THE PERMIAN PERIOD

In some places, for instance Britain, the coal-bearing strata of the Carboniferous period are followed by barren sandstones, and the Permian rocks are as notable for their tendency towards reddish-coloured sands and marls, denoting a thin or non-existent vegetation cover, as the Carboniferous rocks are for their coal measures. The general pattern of life other than that of the plants, however, was similar to that in the Carboniferous, thus justifying the inclusion of the Permian in the Palaeozoic era. Amphibians continued: the reptiles, however, were much more commonly to be found. A transitional form, *Seymouria*, from Seymour (Texas) had a remarkable combination of amphibian and reptile characteristics, but, like the platypus, it seems to be a relic of the original transitional forms rather than a transitional form itself, since its Lower Permian age comes after the reptiles of the Carboniferous. Also living in the Permian were the Cotylosauria, the group of reptiles from which all other reptiles can be considered to be derivative.

The amphibians are little more than land-adapted fish, and usually obliged to return to the water at some stage in their life-cycles, if only to lay their eggs. Indeed, the Mexican axolotl will, if given an artificially heavy dose of the hormone, thyroxin, when it is in its aquatic larval form, become a land-dwelling, air-breathing creature; otherwise, it may remain gilled even at the breeding stage. The reptiles are truly land animals, except where they have re-adapted themselves to the water, e.g. ichthyosaurs and sea snakes. The fish and amphibian practice of developing a set of palatal teeth within the outer set was retained to some extent by the reptiles.

From the Cotylosauria developed the Permian members of the Synapsida, which include the ancestors of our existing mammals.

THE END-PERMIAN CHANGE OF LIFE

It cannot be said that the catastrophe which befell the living world at the end of the Permian interfered very much with the general pattern of reptile evolution. The Carboniferous flora seems to have made a gradual changeover to a new régime of mainly gymnosperm plants during Permian times, so that the transition to the Triassic Period was not a sharply-defined event in floral history. In the invertebrate world, however, the end of the Permian Period was the end of many major groups—all the trilobites, and many types of cephalopods, echinoderms, corals, and various other groups became extinct; hence the Triassic Period is assigned to the Mesozoic Era. Indeed, many reptilian families died out at this juncture, though, as mentioned above, the larger groups generally had a few representatives which survived and provided for a re-expansion in the Triassic Period. The cause of this mass-extinction is not known for certain, but it seems to coincide with a temporary world-wide lowering of the sea-level. Further consideration of this startling interruption in the history of life, is given in the next chapter.

6 The Mesozoic World

'The conclusion is inescapable that the Arctic Ocean in the Jurassic had no ice cap and that its waters were at least as warm as those of the present temperate zones.' – Arkell (Jurassic Geology of the World: 1956)

The dawn of the Mesozoic Era was marked by the recovery of the animal world, but it was a world markedly different from what had existed before. The corals were represented by the new types existing today, capable of forming large-scale colonies and destined to be a far greater factor in reef-formation than the Palaeozoic corals ever had been. The crinoids and brachiopods dwindled in importance, but the molluscs progressed rapidly. Prominent among the new Mesozoic mollusc types were the oysters with their cemented life (one of the commonest marine fossils of post-Palaeozoic rocks) and the advanced ammonoids. The history of the Ammonoidea is rather complex, but suffice it to say that the small, rotund goniatites with their simple sutures (sutures are the lines where diaphragm-like septa join onto the wall of the ammonoid skeleton) arose in the Devonian and were supplanted in the Triassic by the larger, more complex-sutured ceratites. Finally, the very complex-sutured ammonites took over in importance in the Jurassic and Cretaceous periods. Fig. 26 illustrates these facts diagrammatically (the thickness of the curving black column indicates the approximate number of fossils to be found).

Among the vertebrates there were few major changes in the general situation, despite the decimations of the Palaeozoic/Mesozoic disaster. However, two groups, of minor importance in the Mesozoic Era but with a great importance for the future, arose: the mammals and the birds. Among the plants, the Palaeozoic flora was slowly replaced by the Cycadophyte flora: Cycadophytes resembled modern cycads, which are plants with small, hard, woody stems growing extremely slowly (a foot every 200 years in some species), and palm-like foliage springing directly from the stem.

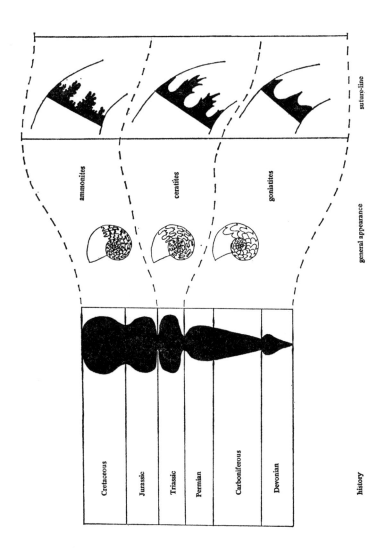

history   general appearance   suture-line

Cretaceous

Jurassic

Triassic

Permian

Carboniferous

Devonian

ammonites

ceratites

goniatites

Fig. 26   *The Ammonoidea*

THE TRIASSIC SITUATION

In the Triassic the ray-fin fish began to take to the sea, and the rival fish groups were by then reduced to minor rôles, as is the case today. On the land, however, the situation was quite different from the present time, and the dominant vertebrate group was the Reptilia, chief among which were the Archosauria (dinosaurs etc.), a position which they held till the close of the Cretaceous, a total span of over 100,000,000 years. The Archosauria developed an extraordinary variety of types in the Mesozoic Era, but were mainly represented by early types in the Triassic; for example the phytosaurs, which were closely connected with the crocodiles in form (sharp teeth, long snout, raised nostrils, stubby limbs), although they did not lead to the crocodiles in evolution, and presumably had the same ecology as the crocodiles in accordance with the general principle that, if there is a niche to be filled, evolution will do its best to fill it, even though the 'proper' animal is not yet available. In accordance with this general principle, one finds among the Triassic ray-fin fish, *Colobodus*, looking like a cod; *Dollopterus*, looking like a flying fish; *Cleithrolepis* and *Bobastrania*, like sunfish; *Saurichthys* and *Birgeria*, like pikes; and *Thoracopterus* like a flying fish. Presumably the ecologies of these pairs correspond to at least some extent, though they are not at all closely connected in evolution. The Triassic coelocanths, on the other hand, resembled modern *Latimeria* because of a genuine genetic relationship.

As for the invertebrate world, the Triassic is notable for the proliferation of shell-banks of oysters and the spread of ceratites. The latter, illustrated by Fig. 26, are ammonoids with moderately complex sutures, and are remarkable for their great variety of shapes and size. Indeed, this sudden success of the Ammonoidea after their near-extinction at the end of the Permian Period is only paralleled by the equally sudden success of the Ammonoidea after their near-extinction at the end of the Triassic Period. This manic-depressive tendency on the part of the ammonoids seems to characterize the group generally, and the sudden appearance and disappearance of certain types of ammonoids throughout the Mesozoic Era is an invaluable clue to the age of the rocks investigated. The *Treatise of Invertebrate Palaeontology* lists 30 ammonoid zones for the Triassic of Western Europe (compared with about 45 for the Jurassic and 36 for the Cretaceous). Each of these zones is characterized by its ammonoids which the specialist can identify and hence estimate the age of the rock containing them.

THE JURASSIC–CRETACEOUS SITUATION

Among the vertebrates, the reptile world became dominated by the Archosauria (including the flying Pterosauria, the aquatic crocodiles, the herbivorous Ornithischia and the sometimes gigantic Saurischia), with ichthyosaurs and plesiosaurs invading the sea, and early turtles, lizards, and snakes. Simultaneously with this ascendancy of the reptiles, however, the seeds of their own successors were sown, as two warm-blooded offshoots developed from the main reptilian stocks; the birds (beginning in the Jurassic) and the mammals (indistinctly beginning in the Triassic, and more definitely in the later Mesozoic). However, there is little evidence that these new groups presented any more of a threat to the reptiles than the bats of today do to the birds. It might have seemed in Upper Cretaceous times that the reptiles would hold their position for ever. As we now know, they did not, and they have sunk into decline.

The plant world changed drastically during the Cretaceous Period. Until the Upper Cretaceous, the Cycadophyte flora was developing a fairly rich cover of cycad-like plants, ginkgos, conifers, and ferns. Cycads are described on page 92, conifers are familiar today as fir, pine, etc., while the ginkgo of modern parks and gardens is a relic of an ancient and nearly extinct group. The ginkgos are gymnosperm trees, formerly very widespread, but dwindling until a short time ago; they survived in sacred Japanese gardens from which they have now spread in large numbers.

This Cycadophyte flora was suddenly overtaken during the course of the Cretaceous Period by the Angiosperm flora (flowering plants), which apparently spread rapidly from Greenland to all parts of the world. Grass is, of course, an angiosperm, so familiar to us today that a world without it is almost inconceivable, yet there was presumably no grass before the Cretaceous Period. The Greenland Cretaceous flora, moreover, includes plants very much like those of today—plane, breadfruit, magnolia and oak are all represented by similar genera. It is very difficult to explain this sudden development of the plants; insects may have been a factor, but these have a history dating back into the Palaezoic Era. Nor does the rise of the angiosperms coincide with the disappearance of the dinosaurs, nor with the exceptionally low sea-level at the end of the Cretaceous (which could have promoted the spread of land plants across formerly flooded straits).

Among the invertebrates, a rich coral-mollusc fauna developed, the widespread distribution of which has led to the supposition that either the poles were warmer in those days, or they lay over open

ocean and hence left no evidence of ice-scratchings on the rock.
This matter is as yet unresolved, but at any rate the world of
which we have evidence seems to have been a warm, equable place
in the Mesozoic Era, and in the tropical regions of the world there
developed marine bivalves which are unknown after the Cretaceous
Period. These include the rudists, a type of bivalve sometimes of
great size (up to 5 ft tall), usually cemented on to the sea-floor, and
sometimes very numerous. These rudists are mostly limited to
regions of the Earth along the present north Tropic, and if their
large size and abundance is a reliable guide to high temperature,
this may represent the Cretaceous equatorial region. Occasional
rudists are found as far north as England, but most of the rocks
containing them in great numbers ocur in the Alpine-Himalayan
regions of the Earth, an area which was formerly occupied by the
ocean Tethys (now pushed up to form mountains), significantly a
little north of the present-day equator.

THE CEPHALOPODS

Class Cephalopoda
   Subclass Nautiloidea
   Subclass Ammonoidea
      Order Goniatitina ('goniatites')
      Order Ceratitina ('ceratites')
      Order Ammonitina ('ammonites')
      (+ other orders)
   Subclass Coleoidea
      Order Belemnoidea
      (+ other orders)

Of all the fossils characteristic of the Jurassic and Cretaceous
Periods, the ammonites and belemnites are probably the most
familiar to amateurs and students. Belemnites are the bullet-shaped
counterweights (see Fig. 8) of solid calcite belonging to squid-like
cephalopods. The creature which owned the belemnite enveloped it
completely, and the impressions of soft parts on the outside of the
belemnite prove this. One might expect the belemnoids to have
been good swimmers, as their descendants, the squids and cuttlefish,
are; and indeed this seems to have been so.

   Ammonites are much-collected fossils—even by amateurs with no
theoretical background—because of their great beauty and spiral
symmetry. The brassy iron pyrites casts, and coloured calcite specimens, are particularly coveted. However, the theoretical light that

they shed on Mesozoic history is of much greater significance to the serious student of this particular department of palaeontology.

It has already been explained (p. 92) how ammonites are related to the general cephalopod structure, and how they—as well as the ceratites and goniatites—are useful for zoning purposes (pp. 93–94). In effect, the ammonoids have the four properties required of a zoning fossil:

(a) it should be easily recognizable
(b) it should evolve rapidly
(c) it should be widespread geographically
(d) it should be numerous

Ammonoids can often be identified even from fragments, since their whorl-section, sculpture and suture is often continued predictably throughout the shell; they evolve rapidly and recognizably, occur throughout the world from the Devonian Period to the Cretaceous Period, and are often very numerous. Their defects, compared with other fossils, are slight, but must also be mentioned. Certain of them evolve slowly, homoeomorphy occurring when, by sheer exhaustion of the variety of shapes available to them, types widely separated in evolution come to look similar. Moreover they are limited to marine rocks (although by no means all of them), and can be surprisingly scarce, for no obvious reason. The zones based on ammonites can be remarkably accurate, and in localities where sedimentation has been slow one can sometimes see how zones which are hundreds of feet thick some miles away may be condensed to a few inches of rock. Under these circumstances the condensed squence may contain ammonites cut in half by erosion surfaces within the rock, and a danger arises here in that ammonites may be excavated from unconsolidated rocks by erosion and laid down in newer sediment, thus providing false age information for the later sediment. This contingency, however, can be guarded against by watching for the characteristically worn appearance of such 'derived' fossils.

Ammonite zones are quoted by the names of the chosen typical species: thus *Psiloceras planorbis* characterizes the Planorbis zone of the Lower Jurassic. It might be assumed from this that a geologist descending from his helicopter (or camel) in some little-known desert will be bound to find *Psiloceras planorbis* if he has landed on the Planorbis zone. This is seldom the case, however; if the rock is exposed, and is marine, and is not of a too shallow-water or deep-water type, he may indeed find this fossil, but he may very likely find its contemporary ammonites without finding *Psiloceras planorbis* itself. Unless he is himself a specialist in ammonites, he

D

may very well prefer to reserve judgement till he has consulted the literature and/or a specialist on the subject, and in so doing he may employ the 'faunal assemblage' method—if A, B, C, D, E, and F occur with Z at one place, and Z is the zoning fossil, the occurrence of A, C, E, and F at another place suggests very strongly that the latter is in the Z-zone. A, B, C, D, E, and F may all be ammonites, but they could be other fossils. Generally, fossils other than ammonoids are less easy to use for stratigraphic purposes, and many are virtually useless on account of slow evolution, and so on.

Mention should also be made of the ammonites which do not provide useful stratigraphic information. Amongst these are the 'smooth dwarfs', certain rather smooth, featureless ammonites which look the same whichever age they are. There are also the uncoiled types which, perhaps because some of them were crawlers rather than swimmers, are less useful for zoning than the flat-spiral types. The flat-spiral types were, if the interpretation is correct, swimmers like the fish of today. A hint of how they lived can be gained by the study of the modern *Nautilus*, which, though it is not an ammonite, is related to them and structurally similar. *Nautilus* rests on the sea-floor during the day, swimming by jet-propulsion (like the squids, cuttlefish and octopus), seizing its prey with its tentacles, but not using the tentacles for locomotion. The gas-filled shell serves to keep the *Nautilus* upright, but does not cause it to float. This swimming propensity contributes strongly towards the ammonoids' usefulness as zoning fossils: an animal that swims or floats across the world is much likely to be widespread geographically than a crawler, which is constantly encountering ecological barriers.

This analogy of *Nautilus* with the ammonoids is a clue to the latter's evolution of the septa. A cephalopod with a gas-filled shell which dives deep or rises through a great height in the sea, at any speed, is likely to collapse or explode, respectively, unless its shell is strongly built. The early ammonoids, with their sutures not much more complex than *Nautilus*'s, were at a disadvantage in this respect since, the suture being the outside outline of the septum, the septum was weakly connected to the wall of the shell and so easily broken. Progression via the ceratite condition to the ammonite condition, however, was achieved by fluting the edges of the septa more and more, and so giving the shell a stronger construction, just as a girder is stronger than a simple strip of iron. It is perhaps a little surprising, therefore, that the ammonoids vanished for ever with the passing of the Cretaceous Period, while the *Nautilus* is still with us—however, water-pressure is hardly likely to have been the only ecological factor at work.

THE MESOZOIC REPTILES

Class Reptilia
  Subclass Anapsida
    Order Chelonia (turtles)
    Order Cotylosauria
    (+ another order)
  Subclass Lepidosauria
    Order Squamata (lizards)
    Order Rhynchocephalia
    (+ another order)
  Subclass Archosauria
    Order Thecodontia
    Order Crocodilia (crocodiles)
    Order Pterosauria (flying reptiles)
    Order Saurischia   ⎫
    Order Ornithischia ⎬ (dinosaurs)
  Subclass Euryapsida (plesiosaurs, etc.)
  Subclass Ichthyopterygia (ichthyosaurs)
  Subclass Synapsida (mammal-like reptiles)
  (See Fig. 27)

The dinosaurs, as commonly understood, are the great reptiles of the Mesozoic Era and are mainly Saurischia and Ornithischia— that is, the reptiles with a lizard-type pelvis or a bird-like pelvis respectively. This may seem a trivial difference, in view of the fact that creatures like the turtle have developed whole new sets of bones for their own purposes, and snakes have reduplicated units, like ribs, almost indefinitely. But it is a difference which is found to hold good for these two different types of archosaurs, and so is illustrated here (Fig. 28). The Ornithischia were herbivorous, and exhibit a great variety of specialized types: *Hypsilophodon* was of monkey-size, and had long toes which may possibly suggest a monkey-like arboreal mode of life. *Iguanodon*, the first dinosaur to be recognized for what it was, was a large reptile with a spike- like thumb—an early representation of this creature, not quite sure what to do with the spiky bone, put it on the end of its nose!

The hadrosaurs were duck-billed, and most presumably fed in a manner analogous to that of the modern ducks. Fossils from North America have the skin preserved as well as the bones, and webbed

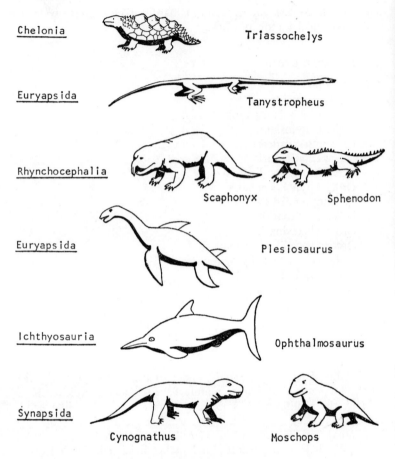

Chelonia — Triassochelys

Euryapsida — Tanystropheus

Rhynchocephalia — Scaphonyx, Sphenodon

Euryapsida — Plesiosaurus

Ichthyosauria — Ophthalmosaurus

Synapsida — Cynognathus, Moschops

Fig. 27 *Mesozoic reptiles other than the Archosaurs*
also showing Sphenodon (recent)

fingers are in evidence, thus extending the resemblance to ducks further, though there seems to have been no webs for the toes. It was at one time suggested that the various types of bony crest to be seen in hadrosaur skulls were secondary sexual characteristics —the males had crests, the females did not. However, this seems unlikely since a careful study of the hadrosaurs reveals that these two types are of different geological ages, thus making the reproduction of these reptiles highly problematical, to say the least.

The stegosaurs include a reptile remarkable for its tiny brain

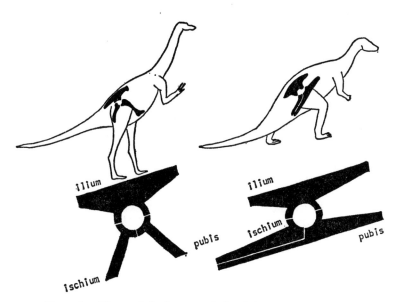

Fig. 28   *The pelvic bones of the Dinosaurs and their*
relationship to classification

size, but it boosted this by having an additional nerve centre in its rear quarters. *Stegosaurus* seems to have tried to solve its defence problems by developing a double row of plates along its back and a bunch of spikes on its tail; the ankylosaurs by developing a coating of bony armour so that the reptile must have looked like a giant armadillo, complete with a heavy mace-like tail, while *Triceratops* developed a three-horned rhinoceros-like skull (except that the rhinoceros's horn is felted hair rather than bone).

Saurischia were variously herbivorous and carnivorous: there was a strong tendency towards the two-legged habit in this group, and in fact some of the smaller types were so well-adapted to running that their bones were hollow for added weight-saving, a feature usually associated with the birds (though one would expect a reptile's movements to be sudden and brief like a crocodile's rather than sustained like an ostrich's). The larger flesh-eating dinosaurs were also two-legged but more massively built. The largest land carnivores on earth belonged to this group, including the famous *Tyrannosaurus* with its four-foot long jaws bristling with five-inch long teeth, and its tiny, apparently useless forelegs. The herbivorous Saurischia were no less remarkable, and included the world's largest land animals (*Diplodocus* was c. 90 ft long including a very long whip-like tail), *Apatosaurus* (= *Brontosaurus*) 70 ft long and 30 tons in weight, and *Brachiosaurus* (estimated 80 ft long and 50 tons in weight).

The vertebrae of these great reptiles were hollowed-out in part to relieve the burden on the legs; nevertheless the weight of some of them may have been prohibitive to sustained life on land, and it has been suggested that they waded in water and kept their heads above water-level by means of their long, snake-like necks. A simple mathematical relationship can illustrate this problem of support in large animals: the tiny flea can jump many times its own height on the frailest of legs, while the elephant requires pillar-like limbs to keep its weight up. Elephants may charge, but they do not jump. Consider the flea: if each of its linear dimensions is doubled, its volume (and hence its weight) is increased eight-fold, while the cross-sectional area of its legs (and hence their strength) is only raised four-fold. Thus the giant man-eating spiders of horror fiction are hardly likely to disturb the philosophical mind, since such creatures would break their legs under their own weight.

The very large reptiles would have been greatly aided by a watery environment to reduce the weight of their bodies. In confirmation of this, one can quote the nostrils of *Brachiosaurus*, which are elevated above the rest of the skull, apparently for breathing air while the animal was under water, as in the hippopotamus and crocodile of today. It has been observed, however, that the tracks in the Paluxy River Cretaceous of Texas indicate that these great animals could walk with their weight on the legs (i.e. with little or no buoyancy from water), without collapsing. Furthermore, the water-pressure on the body of any animal, more than a few feet below the surface, prevents it from breathing through its emergent nostrils; otherwise, there would be no need for diving suits, since one could use long snorkels for deep-diving. It would appear, therefore, that the reconstruction showing the great herbivorous dinosaurs as aquatic creatures must be viewed with caution.

There were other archosaurs besides these, moreover: the Crocodilia was a prominent group, and still is widespread today, retaining some very ancient features, such as the bony armour plates on the back. In Jurassic times the known crocodiles seem to have been marine. Some Mesozoic crocodiles evidently became very tiny (as little as 1 ft long), but it is questionable to what extent they resembled modern crocodiles in their habits, since the latter prefer

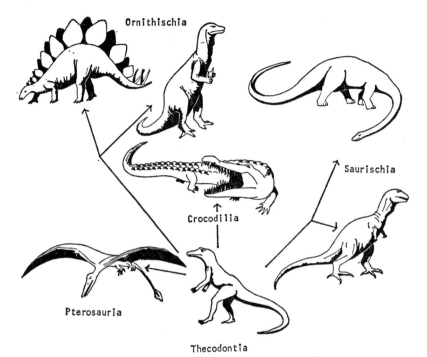

Ornithischia

Saurischia

Crocodilia

Pterosauria

Thecodontia

Fig. 29   *Evolution of the Archosauria*
(not to scale)

to seize their prey with a sudden rush, and drown it by holding it under water in their powerful jaws. For this purpose a secondary palate is needed in the roof of the mouth, to enable the crocodile to breathe while the jaw-line is submerged. The Jurassic crocodiles do not have this secondary palate well developed, though it may have been present as a soft palate. *Phobosuchus* (Cretaceous) had a skull 6 ft long, the whole animal being perhaps 45 ft long (c.f. the modern maximum of c. 33 ft).

Some of the archosaurs (Pterosauria) took to the air, developing a wing of skin attached to a greatly developed fourth finger, though the construction of the skeleton suggests a gliding and soaring mode of life rather than the complicated wing-beating of the bats and birds. The grotesque and often tooth-filled jaw and huge eyes added to their exotic appearance, and *Pteranodon* (wingspan up to 25 ft) also had a large postcranial crest. Other archosaurs which took to the air developed the feathered wing, and so became birds (see below). It can thus be seen that archosaurs invaded practically every environment available, though they were not particularly successful in the sea, probably because this niche was already filled by other reptiles—mainly the ichthyosaurs and plesiosaurs.

The ichthyosaurs had a porpoise-like body, and a reptilian jaw. Most of the swimming action seems to have been achieved by the body and tail, the paddles serving as steering devices. The eyes were very large and contained bony supports. Some well-preserved specimens show a viviparous type of birth, thus freeing the animal entirely from its land connections. The plesiosaurs, on the other hand, propelled themselves through the water by means of their large-paddle-like feet, with a small head on the end of a long, snake-like neck. The stomach contents of fossil plesiosaurs sometimes include smoothed pebbles which were presumably swallowed by the animals for the purpose of grinding up tough food material. Other marine reptiles include the true marine lizards of the Cretaceous Period and the modern sea-snakes. Snakes are, on the whole, more typical of the Cenozoic than the Mesozoic eras, and appear to be descended from primitive lizards.

Three Mesozoic reptile groups remain to be mentioned: the Chelonia (turtles) and Synapsida (mammal-like reptiles), and Rhynchocephalia. The Chelonia, though familiar today in the form of tortoises and turtles, are in many ways extraordinary reptiles. Their skeletal structure is basically of the normal reptilian type, but on top of and underneath this internal skeleton is an armour of bony plates, which are further strengthened by an external armour (the plates of which seldom correspond exactly with the bony armour, since this would weaken the system) of horny plates—tortoiseshell, useful in jewellery and other ornamental work, is from this last-mentioned part. One may well wonder how these armour bones, and, indeed, how the chelonian skeleton as a whole arose. The earliest recognizable chelonians, e.g. *Triassochelys* (Triassic), bear witness to their cotylosaurian ancestry. *Triassochelys* still has teeth (later Chelonia lost them), and it is doubtful whether turtles of this type could withdraw their head and tail limbs completely into their shell, but already the armour had formed, and the internal skeleton was fixed to it. Later chelonians have proved both diverse and numerous. Some grew to a large size (*Testudo atlas*, Pliocene, was about 8 ft long). Some turtles took to an aquatic life, and some were even marine (though they have to breathe air, of course, like all other reptiles). The group has not been deterred by the rise of the mammals since the Mesozoic time.

The Rhynchocephalia are remarkable in that one species survives today—*Sphenodon* (the 'tuatara')—though the group is mainly Mesozoic. It is fortunate that we have the tuatara to convey the living appearance of a member of an otherwise fossil group; it is a small lizard-like creature living on the islands off New Zealand. One curiosity of *Sphenodon* is its still functional pineal 'eye', a light-sensitive organ on the top of the head, inherited from the fishes, and additional to two normal eyes.

The Synapsida was a large and mainly Permian–Triassic group with early forms including *Dimetrodon*, the famous sail-back reptile (the sail's function not being definitely understood), and—at the Triassic/Jurassic boundary—the Ictidosauria, a group of reptiles whose relationship with the mammals is of great interest and has already been mentioned on pages 24–26.

Summarizing the reptilian history in the Mesozoic Era, one may say that a widespread conquest of the three basic environments of earth, air and water was achieved. This conquest was probably not quite as widespread as the mammals' deployment today, since reptiles, having little or no internal temperature-regulation, become sluggish and weak in low temperatures where mammals and birds can live unperturbed. However, the structure of the ribs in certain of the Synapsida suggests a capacity for rhythmic breathing which could signify the constant temperature-regulation normally associated with mammals and birds, and since the reptiles are plainly the ancestors of both birds and mammals—and hence man— they can fairly be said to be responsible for the state of the non-aqueous world as it is today. Many of them are very large : 15–20 ft long is 'medium-sized' for the Archosauria. Some of them were very bizarre in their structure. Most reptilian skeletons can be assigned to a particular mode of life from a study of the skeletal structure, but some are rather baffling. It is difficult, for example, to think of any mode of life for *Tanystropheus*, with its snake-like neck— the neck vertebrae differ so markedly from the body vertebrae that the skeleton was originally ascribed to two different animals. It is also difficult to see how some of the flying reptiles managed to get off the ground, if they ever landed on it, with their slender, grasping, hind legs, unless they rested in the bats' position, head-downwards, suspended from a rock or branch. Perhaps, like the modern albatross, they landed as rarely as possible.

It would hardly be complete to conclude the subject of the Mesozoic reptiles without some mention of Professors Marsh and Cope in nineteenth-century U.S.A., whose rivalry in the field of dinosaur-excavation must have enlivened the palaeontological world of that time, ranging as it did from publishing insulting letters about each other to a pitched battle, between their opposing parties, in the field.

OTHER MESOZOIC VERTEBRATES

In the Mesozoic Era, however, the reptiles were not the only vertebrates abroad. Apart from the fish and amphibians, there were the new classes of Aves (birds) and Mammalia (mammals). The origin of the birds has been mentioned on page 29; once established, the birds slowly took over from the reptiles in the Cretaceous Period. In terms of their skeletons, birds are very conservative, and retain reptilian characteristics in a modified form. It is interesting to note that as early as the Cretaceous a bird (*Hesperornis*) with reduced wings showed a tendency to flightlessness.

The mammals were no quicker than the birds to establish their position. The first mammals were Middle-Upper Jurassic (depending on one's interpretation of the word 'mammal'), and the next time the fossil record reveals them is in the Upper Cretaceous, when they are still insignificant compared with their reptilian neighbours. It is regrettable that the quaint, egg-laying platypus and echidna of Australasia have virtually no known fossil history: it is assumed from their primitive, partially reptilian structure that they have an origin somewhere in the early Mesozoic. The rest of the mammal world today can be summed up as the marsupials (pouched mammals, e.g. kangaroo) and placentals (mammals with a placenta in childbirth, forming the majority of living mammals, including man); both date back to the Upper Cretaceous, the marsupials being then probably more numerous than the placentals.

A glimpse of the mid-Mesozoic mammalian situation (which also serves to emphasize the imperfections of the fossil record by the great scarcity of mammal fossils in the Lower Cretaceous Period) is provided by the Upper Jurassic. At the Isle of Purbeck, in England, a pocket of mammalian remains was found in the Upper Jurassic rocks. The mammals were evidently small, of the order of a foot in length. Some seem to have been carnivorous (one apparently paralleled modern rodents in its dentition), and to have climbed trees, no doubt to gnaw the bark and fruits. Whether these creatures laid eggs or not is not certainly known, but the skeletal evidence suggests that these mammals had advanced beyond this stage. The fossil soil associated with this discovery was optimistically named the 'Mammal Bed', to the annoyance of undergraduates on field work, since virtually no mammal remains have been found in it since 1856. None of the Jurassic mammals so far discussed belongs to any of the three groups alive today, and only one of them (notable for rodent-like teeth), survived till the early Tertiary Era. All were small in size, no doubt to avoid the attentions of the great carnivorous reptiles.

FOSSIL INSECTS

It should perhaps first be emphasized that, while fossil vertebrates are very numerous in terms of species (there are in fact nearly as many fossil vertebrate species known as living ones), it is the invertebrates which are, as a general rule, most commonly found as fossils because of the large number of individual specimens the invertebrates provide. One would perhaps expect the insects, which exceed the rest of the animal world combined in terms of numbers of species alive today, to be equally prolific in the fossil record, but—despite their hard outer casing—their small size and frailty militate against their capacity for fossilization, and in fact the number of fossil insect species quoted for any particular time in geological history may not be so much a reflection of insect abundance or diversity at that time, as a reflection of the occurrence of conveniently-exposed insect-bearing strata. The radical elements of insect evolution took place in the Palaezoic Era, and the Mesozoic Era was probably a time of development on themes already begun.

THE END OF THE MESOZOIC ERA

The most striking question arising from a survey of the Mesozoic is—why did Mesozoic life come to such a catastrophic end as it did at the end of the Cretaceous? It would be as well to say at once that no one really knows the answer. When one is dealing with materials, such as bones and shells, it is relatively easy to ascertain the answer to a certain problem by direct research, but the question of mass-extinction is not susceptible to direct description and deduction. Too many factors, such as the inter-relationships of animals, climate, and so on have left too little record for the answer to such a fundamental question to be readily given. The horse (*Equus*) is present in the American Quaternary, where it died out and subsequently flourished when re-introduced by the white man, a phenomenon difficult to explain despite its relatively recent date. Theories concerning the extinction of dinosaurs are legion, and include such extravaganzas as: ferns are commoner in the Mesozoic than the Tertiary, ferns are well-known for their laxative properties, therefore the dinosaurs all died of constipation! Concentrating on the facts as we know them, the following points relevant to the problem may be stated.

(a) though the dinosaurs became quite extinct at the end of the Cretaceous, they were only accompanied by certain of the reptiles; some reptile groups had already gone (for example, the ichthyosaurs), while others survived into the Cenozoic and indeed to the present day (lizards, turtles, crocodiles, Rhynchocephalia). The plesiosaurs and pterosaurs, however, died out with the dinosaurs.

(b) the birds and mammals did not die out at the end of the Mesozoic.

(c) in the sea, only certain groups were affected. The ammonites, belemnoids and rudist bivalves died out, but the other bivalves, the gastropods, corals, echinoderms, nautiloids, Bryozoa and so on, survived. The fish were not greatly affected by the end-Cretaceous boundary.

(d) the plants show no profound changes at this time. The great expansion of the flowering plants was already thoroughly established by then.

Nevertheless, the sudden disappearance of so many forms of Mesozoic life at the same time requires explanation. It is of interest to consider the sediments themselves at this time. When one visits the quarries and cliffs exposing these rocks, one finds that very often the continental shelf marine sediments become non-marine, or retire modestly into an unconformity so that the critical strata are missing altogether. A continuous marine sequence is of great value in studying the changes between Mesozoic and Tertiary times (since non-marine fossils tend to be sporadic and difficult to date accurately), but such a sequence is usually to be found in deep-water sediments, where fossils are rare. Examples are known, however, of fairly continuous continental shelf marine sedimentation, and the change of life is clearly seen in them.

The same problems of the Mesozoic/Tertiary boundary occur with the Palaeozoic/Mesozoic boundary, and workers on the few continuous marine Permian–Triassic transition sequences have remarked on the sudden changes in the major animal groups. Whatever explanation is offered for the change of life at the boundaries, it must account for the above-mentioned facts; no single explanation seems to have won general favour, but it would appear that the mammals of the Tertiary developed to fill a vacuum left behind by the demise of the reptiles, and it was not a case of the rising up in arms of the mammals against the reptiles and defeating them. Possibly some readjustment of the Earth's interior caused the ocean floors (or one of them) to sag a little, thus causing the water to depart from the continental shelves, which might kill off the life dependent on the shelf, though it is not entirely clear how this would affect life on the land.

The Universe is generally assumed to be static, but we have no guarantee of this. The eruption of a supernova star (that is, a star which suddenly increases its luminosity as it explodes) within our part of the galaxy might produce unpleasant radiation effects similar to those of a nuclear war (though these would, of course, be weakened by passage through water). The last supernova in our galaxy exploded in 1604 A.D., fortunately not too near, though near enough to be visible to the naked eye. Presumably other, nearer, supernova have, at various times in the past, exposed our planet to the blast of subatomic particles. The supernova of 1054 A.D., recorded in the Far East, was visible during daylight. Astronomers, studying the distribution of hydrogen in our galaxy, have found a shell of gas exploding towards the Earth at 33 miles per second, apparently the relic of an explosion 30,000,000 years ago. The hydrogen may be infinitesimally thinned by the time it reaches us, but the flash (which would have arrived after a mere 30,000 years) and the subatomic particles (which would have arrived shortly after the light) may have been quite strong. The Cretaceous/Tertiary boundary is, however, dated at 60–70 million years ago. The object of this paragraph is to remark that, while one may discount variations in the radiation received from outer space as being negligibly weak in their effects on life on Earth now, one cannot be sure that this was always so in the past.

OTHER EVIDENCE OF MESOZOIC LIFE

Sometimes one encounters, or reads of, fossils which are very evocative of the Mesozoic world. The discovery of a 'nest' of dinosaur eggs in the Gobi Desert by R. C. Andrews's expedition was no doubt such an occasion. Some of the eggs were found to contain the remains of embryos, the reptile which laid them— *Protoceratops*—seems to have been related to the famous triple-horned *Triceratops*. Another such example is the discovery in a German sandstone of large reptile footprints closing in on small insect footprints, and—further along the same trail—the ominous existence of only one (large) set of prints.

7   The Tertiary World

'A camel is a horse designed by a committee' – Anon

The Cenozoic Era is rather arbitrarily divided into two parts—the Tertiary Era and the Quaternary 'Era'. The Quaternary represents just the last 2,000,000 years or so, and only qualifies for separate consideration on account of the large surface area of its thin but important sediments. Its duration is roughly comparable with a couple of Mesozoic ammonite zones. The Tertiary Era, which precedes the Quaternary, is of more appreciable duration (70,000,000 years), and the Cenozoic as a whole may be described as the age of mammals.

The dimunition of Mesozoic life at the end of the Cretaceous, and the problems associated with it, were discussed in the last chapter. It remains to relate now what the new life that succeeded it was like. One of the central facts of Cenozoic Palaeontology is the consistent if uneven decline in temperature from the early part of the Cenozoic towards the later part. The explanation of this is for the moment deferred, but it is a phenomenon which is repeatedly evident in Cenozoic studies, and it culminates in the Ice Ages of the Quaternary.

INFORMATION PROVIDED BY TERTIARY INVERTEBRATES
AND PLANTS

With the sudden decline of the ammonoids and belemnoids at the end of the Cretaceous, the only cephalopods left to continue the habitation of the sea, apart from the last remaining associates of *Nautilus*, were the descendants of the belemnoids—the squids, octopus, cuttlefish, and so on. No doubt these would provide an interesting example of evolutionary development, but the tendency towards shell-reduction is so pronounced in them that their fossil record is very slight compared with the other molluscs. As for the latter, the numbers of bivalves and gastropods are so numerous in Cenozoic rocks that one may well wonder whether the Cenozoic should not be called the age of the bivalves and gastropods. These molluscs seem to have reached their height today, and the size and variety of the modern Indo-Pacific species alone is daunting to a shell-collector with limited storage space. Over 120,000 mollusc species (living and fossil), most of them Cenozoic bivalves and gastropods, are estimated at the present state of knowledge, compared with about 60,000 vertebrate species. Only the insects and plants exceed them: approximately 250,000 plant and 800,000 insect species are believed to be known, and more are constantly being described.

Evolution within the Bivalvia and Gastropoda is well-marked in the fossils, though it is difficult to quote any general trend by the groups themselves. The rudists were extinct by Tertiary times, but their size has been rivalled by the giant clam *Tridacna* (up to 3 ft long, and 300 lb in weight, including soft parts). Adult bivalves have never achieved marked success in the planktonic field, but parts of the modern oceans are teeming with planktonic gastropods—the pteropods (which are herbivorous) and the heteropods (carnivores), the latter often feeding on the former. Pteropod and heteropod oozes form where the shells of these creatures sink to the ocean floor; these shells are rather tiny and frail, but they sometimes occur as fossils. On the whole, however, bivalves and gastropods are bottom-dwellers, and are too confined to their particular environments to be very useful in large-scale stratigraphy, though they provide useful data on the local ecology, of course. Gastropods and bivalves extend this source of ecological information by occurring in non-marine waters, and gastropods have furthermore mastered dry land in the form of snails. True fossil soils with terrestrial shells in situ are not common, however, and frequently the land-snails are found in lake or river sediments into which they have been washed.

Arthropods are occasionally evident in their many forms; crabs and lobsters occur in marine sediments, and insects are sometimes to be found in non-marine rocks. Ostracods, as the bivalved shells of tiny *Crustacea*, are numerous and important in sediments laid down in water, and are much used by micropalaeontologists to provide stratigraphic and ecological information. In these respects they supplement the Foraminifera, one-celled creatures which, despite their simple soft parts, are capable of great variety of shell sculpture, and produce shells up to 11 cms in diameter. The Pyramids of Egypt are built largely of Tertiary foraminiferal limestone, some of the forams therein being plainly visible to the naked eye and were in fact noticed by Herodotus in 5th century B.C.

The latest researches in micropalaeontology, however are making use of the 'nannoplankton'—that is, the fossils of very tiny plank-tonic organisms—which often proves useful stratigraphically even though a high-powered microscope is needed to study them. Corals have been great reef-builders in the Cenozoic Era, but have become more and more restricted to the Indo-Pacific and Caribbean areas, partly owing to the conversion of many of their former marine haunts to dry land by the Alpine orogeny. Echinoderms are more catholic in their distribution, but also reflect a general tendency towards lower latitudes, as times goes on. The deterioration of the Cenozoic climate is well illustrated by the plants: in the Eocene Period, palms flourished in the latitude of London (51° N); by the end of Miocene they had disappeared from central Germany (50° N); in the early Pliocene, from South Germany (48° N); at present they grow south of 40° N. Palms will, of course, grow rather half-heartedly in higher latitudes today, but will not germi-nate without artificial warmth.

In addition to the cooling of the Earth's climate, there was a second major factor at work in the Cenozoic Era; the disappearance and conversion into mountain ranges of Tethys, the ancient ocean which, in Mesozoic times, stretched from what is now Indonesia via the Himalayas and Alps to the Atlantic, with an additional section in Central America (see pp. 58–59 for a description of the last-mentioned area). The Mediterranean of today represents a remnant of this great ocean, and it is curious how this chain of the world's highest mountains includes rocks which were, as proved by fossils, below sea level comparatively recently. For instance, in the Western European Alps, where the French, Italian and Swiss borders meet in the vicinity of Mont Blanc, the study of the fossils in the rocks has yielded the following information:

(1) The sedimentary rocks of the Alps frequently show evidence of having been laid down by the sea, under various depths of water.

(2) The history of the sea under which the Alpine rocks were formed extends from the early Mesozoic to the mid-Tertiary.

(3) The earth-movements responsible for the Alpine structures come to a climax in Cenozoic times.

(4) Many of the Alpine mountains are formed of blocks of sedi-ment which, being tilted by the earth-movements, have slid bodily downhill like great rafts sometimes many cubic miles in size.

This information has been pieced together after painstaking research by geologists. The fossils are not only used to determine
the chronology of events in the Alps, but also to determine the
geography of the Alpine sea at any given time. Thus the Lower
Tertiary is characterized by the presence of nummulites (large
Foraminifera, now extinct), while the depth of the sea and the
proximity of the shoreline can be deduced from various palaeontological data—ostracods, Foraminifera, molluscs, corals, algae, etc.,
all contribute here. From these pieces of information one can see
how the Alps developed out of a part of the Tethys which was
gradually squeezed into a series of ridges and troughs, roughly
comparable with the ridges and troughs of Indonesia (though the
Alps show a comparative lack of volcanic activity). We also see
how these topographical divisions moved northwards as time went
on, until by the end of the Lower Tertiary the land was mostly
emergent from the Tethys, fringed on the north and west sides by
a slender arm of the sea—all that remained of the Alpine sea—and
continually subjected to earthquakes and uplifts to build the great
mountains visible today.

Neither the mountain-building nor the cooling of the climate was
an unprecedented event in the history of the Earth, but what does
mark off the Tertiary Era as being a unique time is the ascendancy
of the Mammalia.

THE TERTIARY BIRDS AND MAMMALS

Although the Tertiary Era is often described as the age of mammals,
it could also be called the age of birds, or the age of gastropods.
for that matter. Birds, however, provide an unsatisfactory fossil
record on account of their frail structure; unlike the mammals, with
their heavy bones and close-to-the-earth living habits. Today the
flightless birds are to some extent restricted to areas where competition from the mammals has been insignificant (e.g. the kiwi of
New Zealand and the Australian cassowary), though birds like the
African ostrich and the South American rhea have used their fast,
elusive running habit to protect them (emus have been recorded at
40 m.p.h.). In the early Tertiary, however, such birds posed a posi-
tive threat to the mammals. *Phororhacos*, standing about 6 ft tall
and possessing a hooked, eagle-like beak a foot long, and an inhabi-
tant of Patagonia as late as the mid-Tertiary, must have been a
creature to be avoided (Fig. 30).

However, the mammals had soon secured a firm position by the
Eocene Period, and in the mid-Tertiary the primitive rhinoceros-type

Fig. 30   *Phororhacos*

Baluchitherium and its relative, *Indricotherium*, set the record for
size among the land-mammals—18 ft high at the shoulder—roughly
the same size as *Tyrannosaurus*, though without the latter's carnivorous qualities (see Fig. 31). Since then the mammals have
flourished in most land habitats, with more modest success in the
air and in water. Their sizes range from the 1½ in long Savi's white-
toothed pygmy shrews, to the 106 ft blue whale, the latter being
the largest animal known, living or fossil.

Fig. 31   *Indricotherium*

MAMMAL CLASSIFICATION

Class Mammalia (familiar examples in brackets)
    Subclass Prototheria
        Order Monotremata (platypus, echidna)
    (+ other subclasses)

Subclass Theria
  Order Marsupialia (kangaroo)
  Order Primates (man, apes)
  Order Insectivora (hedgehog)
  Order Chiroptera (bats)
  Order Artiodactyla (cattle)
  Order Perissodactyla (horses)
  Order Condylarthra
  Order Edentata (sloths)
  Order Cetacea (whales)
  Order Proboscidea (elephants)
  Order Carnivora (cats, dogs)
  Order Rodentia (rats, mice)
  Order Lagomorpha (rabbit)
  (+ other orders)

PRIMATES

In many ways the primates, the order of mammals to which man belongs, is a primitive group. The varied teeth lack the specialization of the more discriminating feeders like the cat or rodent, the five-fingered hand and five-toed foot, which are present in most of the primates, have lost no digits as in the cattle or horse groups. The body of a primate is straightforward, conservatively-designed compared with that of a whale or armadillo. Furthermore, the primate fossil record is rather scantily-distributed, owing to the primates' preference for a tree-dwelling existence in warm climates. Forest floors in warm regions are places of moisture and warmth where decomposition of organic remains is rapid, and bones are less likely to become fossilized there than in river beds or swamps. Indeed, it is this arboreal habitat which has preserved for us the dextrous hands and excellent eyes of the higher primates, since these are essential to an arboreal life. In *The Lost World* by Sir Arthur Conan Doyle, Professor Challenger inquires of Mr Malone whether the ape-man he saw 'could cross its thumb over its palm', a question whose relevance might escape the casual reader; but the Professor was presumably trying to discover whether the creature was in fact a primate. If all four thumbs could be crossed over the four palms, then it would have been a primitive primate of the monkey type. Man, being a more specialized form which has recently taken to land-dwelling, has feet with unopposable big toes.

In the early part of the Tertiary Era the only primates were the prosimians, a group of primitive tree-dwelling creatures represented today by small groups, like the lemurs, which have survived mainly on the island of Madagascar. By the mid-Tertiary, three main types of primates had evolved from this prosimian stock; the South American monkeys, the Old World monkeys, and the Hominoidea (apes and men). The latter are notable for their large brain-cases. The Tertiary history of the Hominoidea is very scantily known, but fragmentary remains from the Old World suggest that the small-brained *Dryopithecus*, parts of which have been found in the Upper Tertiary, is a transitional form, possibly using the upright or semi-upright gait, leading to the modern chimpanzee, gorilla, and man. The further history of the ancestry of man is deferred to the discussion of the Quaternary.

INSECTIVORA

More primitive than the primates, and presumably ancestral to them, and indeed probably ancestral to all placental mammals, is the Order Insectivora. Shrews, moles and hedgehogs represent this order today, though they are rather more specialized now than their ancestors. The Order is first in evidence in the Upper Cretaceous Period; its more extreme members include the modern *Galeopithecus* (the 'flying lemur'), which is apparently an only partially successful attempt to conquer the air, since the creature can only glide between trees on webs of skin extending between its limbs. Although related to neither the squirrels nor the bats (nor, for that matter, the lemurs), *Galeopithecus* provides an interesting illustration of the intermediate behavioural stage between the squirrel habit (leaping from tree to tree) and the bat habit (true flying). Possibly flying reptiles and birds passed through this stage too.

CHIROPTERA

The bats are often insectivorous, and are so similiar structurally to the Insectivora that they must be closely related, though, like the whales, they already show adaptation to their chosen mode of locomotion so early in the Tertiary that the transitional forms from the Insectivora are difficult to find, *Galeopithecus* being too late to qualify for this position. The tiny pelvis in the bats is curiously similar to the pelvis of the flying reptiles. The bats rarely stand, of course, preferring to hang from rocks or branches, but how the flying reptiles, with their inferior wings, managed to maintain a similar mode of life, is problematical. The bat's wing is a web of skin stretched over four enlarged fingers, unlike the bird's wing

118 PALAEONTOLOGY

(feathers on a modified arm and the vestiges of certain digits), or the flying reptile's (skin borne by an enlarged fourth finger).

Most groups of mammals are alive today; with few major groups extinct. The general diversity of mammals is so great that it is difficult to state a general pattern in their evolution such as one might find in, say, the ammonoids. Most mammal groups are represented by small, unspecialized forms in the early Tertiary Era, showing indistinct relationships with the basic insectivorous stock. In the later Tertiary, these groups become more numerous and develop large and bizarre members, though at the present moment a good many groups (the horse, cattle, sloth, whale and carnivore orders) seem to be stationary or in decline.

ARTIODACTYLA

Of the ungulate (hoofed) mammals there are, as most people are aware, two main types today; the even-toed hoof (or cloven hoof) or Artiodactyla group, and the odd-toed hoof (Perissodactyla) group. The Artiodactyla are still fairly numerous—cattle, deer, gazelles and so forth—but the odd-toed orders are mostly extinct, only the Perissodactyla (horses) surviving as a greatly-diminished relic of its former diversity. The earliest Artiodactyla are small, very primitive Eocene fossils which are virtually indistinguishable, except in points of detail, from the Insectivora and Primates. From these arose the pigs and hippopotami, on the one hand, and the ruminants (cattle etc.) on the other. In the mid-Tertiary arose the 'giant pigs', including *Dinohyus* (10 ft long), while on the ruminant side there developed early gazelle-like camels and giraffe-like camels before camels as we know them emerged. Certain Artiodactyla developed extraordinary horns—thus *Synthetoceras* looked reminiscent of the Cretaceous reptile *Triceratops*.

PERISSODACTYLA

The Perissodactyla, on the other hand, are only represented by the horse, tapir and rhinoceros types today. The hippopotamus is, despite the Greek meaning of its name, more of a river-pig than a river-horse. In Eocene times, there were many groups of Perisso-dactyla, including the titanotheres, a group which approached the elephants in size, though—unlike the elephants—they were notice-ably small-brained. Apparently the titanotheres reached their large size a little too soon, for despite their horns and bulk they did not survive the Oligocene Period. The horses themselves have an

interesting and well-documented evolution (see pp. 20–21), beginning with the 10-in high herbivore *Hyracotherium*—which lived,
to judge by its toes, on soft ground, perhaps in forests—and leading
up to the plains-dwelling *Equus* of today. The rhinoceroses have
the distinction of including the biggest land-mammal of all—
Baluchitherium, which, like the great dinosaurs, developed hollow
vertebrae for the sake of lightness. Most early rhinoceroses were
hornless, some may have been river-dwellers like the modern
hippopotamus, and some early rhinoceroses were sometimes slender
and horselike; but these trends seem to have led nowhere.

OTHER HOOFED MAMMALS

Aside from the principal ungulate groups of the Artiodactyla and
Perissodactyla, there are numerous other orders, all extinct and all
seeming to derive their origin from the early Tertiary order
Condylarthra (as also do the Perissodactyla). The ungulates, or
hoofed orders, are herbivorous, but otherwise there is little to
unite them. The Condylarthra exhibit their primitiveness in their
low-crowned teeth which could not eat tough or gritty vegetation
for sustained periods, a problem which also faced the titanotheres.
Some Condylarthra had not even reached the hoofed stage, and bore
claws suggesting an arboreal habitat. However, the derivative orders
speedily showed their tendency towards specialization; *Uintatherium*
was of the size of an elephant, but possessed of a grotesque horned
head. In South America, protected from the intervention of foreign
mammals by the flooding of Panama, numerous ungulate groups
developed which are now extinct and seem, to present-day eyes,
bizarre. Though hoofs were not always developed, homoeomorphy
between these and the Old World mammal groups, frequently
occurred as a natural result of the demand of the environment for
certain mammalian types, regardless of the orders available to
provide them. Thus, South American 'hippopotamus', 'rhinoceros',
'elephant' and 'horse' types appeared, all unrelated to the epony-
mous Old World forms familiar today.

Yet it seems to be a frequent phenomenon that the evolutionary
strength of a group of animals is proportional to the area it develops
in, and the Old World types (which included North America in
their area, but not Australia) soon overcame the South American
types when Panama emerged as a land-bridge, some time during
the Pliocene Period—though there were a few South American
creatures which survived the competition and invaded North
America. Curiously enough, some of those South American groups

were not restricted to the New World in the earliest Tertiary, suggesting that they were survivors in a temporarily cut-off corner of the world rather than completely original developments.

Amongst the more noteworthy South American ungulates was *Toxodon*, of which Darwin said: 'How wonderfully are the different orders, at the present time so well separated, blended together in different points of structure in the Toxodon!' The head and body are like a hippopotamus, while the teeth are like a rhinoceros's in shape and a rodent's in growth. *Astrapotherium* is another curiosity. Its skeleton looks as if someone had designs for a big, rhinoceros-like creature for the front half, but the back half looks as if the designer had lost interest and added a pelvis and rear limbs of very little strength or solidity. Its mode of life is unknown. More easily interpreted is the horse-like *Thoatherium*, which can claim to have outstripped *Equus* in its horse-development, since Thoatherium's single-toed limb has lost more of the vestigial adjacent toes than *Equus* has. But *Thoatherium* can hardly be treated as a super-horse, since its ankles seem to have been too weak to maintain a sustained running action.

Fig. 32   *Giant Sloth (Megatherium)*

EDENTATA

The Edentata includes typically South American animals—the sloth and armadillo are well-known examples—with the teeth reduced in number or absent, and often with long claws. The sloth, whose torpid movements seem to give it an unhurried air even when it is pursued by a jaguar, is presumably related to the giant ground-sloths, which grew up to 18 ft long and had a particularly massive skeleton (see Fig. 32). The armoured Edentata, of which the armadillo is a member, also showed a gigantism tendency. *Glyptodon*, with its huge bony carapace, exhibits a striking homoeo-morphy with the tortoise, and being about 9 ft long must have looked like a living tank.

CETACEA

The whales have a long and well-documented history, as one might expect from aquatic creatures. Unfortunately, the story of their original migration from the land to the sea is as yet unknown to us, since the first fossils (Eocene) already show advanced specializa-tions of their bodies to a whale-like mode of life, though the skulls and teeth are closer to those of their contemporaries on the land than they are to their descendants in the sea. The earliest whales, like most land-dwellers who have invaded the sea, were carnivorous, and some had fierce-looking jaws and teeth and a total length of 70 ft. Porpoises belong to this group, but the seals are of the Order Carnivora (discussed below), whereas the manatees are of yet a third order, the Sirenia, of which the Eocene members bear distinct traces of their terrestrial origin, including functional hind legs.

PROBOSCIDEA

The elephants hold a very prominent place in the Cenozoic Mam-malia, though today they are represented by only the Indian and African elephants. The proboscidean tusk is a true tooth, and the group has produced a remarkable assortment of tusks in addition to the gently curved type familiar in modern elephants (Fig. 33). It is by no means easy to account for the functions of all these varieties of tusk, but at least some may have been used for plough-ing up ground in search of food, rather like some pigs today, when they root for food with their snouts.

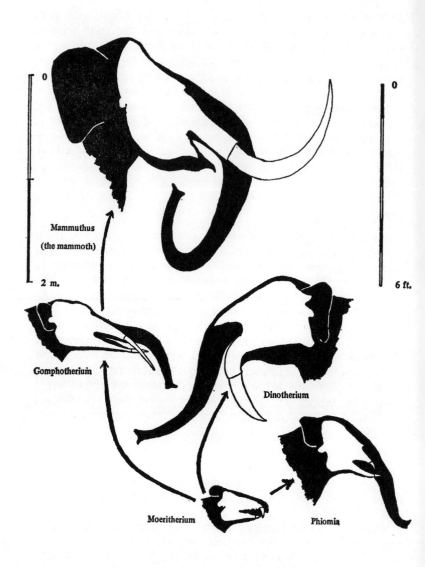

Fig. 33   *Diversification in the Elephants (Order Proboscidea)*
The arrows do not represent the exact course of evolution

CARNIVORA

The Carnivora includes most carnivorous mammals of the Cenozoic; seals, sea-lions, bears, pandas, cats, dogs, hyaenas, weasels and civets all belong to this group. The seals, unlike the whales and ichthyosaurs (which use or used their tails), but like the plesiosaurs, depend on their limbs to act as paddles for motion, the tail being too weak and small to be useful in this respect. Unlike the whales, which date back at least to the Middle Eocene and are even then well-adapted to aquatic life, the seal history cannot be traced back beyond the Miocene. Earlier carnivores are known, of course, but it is inevitably difficult to find fossils of the half-way stage between land and water, when evolution must have been rather rapid at such a profound environmental change. The bears, which include the largest living carnivore (Kodiak bear, 8 ft long or more), are also of indistinct origin, but structural considerations indicate that they are closely related to the dogs.

The dogs have a long and well-documented history, especially in North America, including some very large types. The cats, too, have a distinctive history. In general one may summarize this by saying that the earliest cats were generally of the sabre-tooth type with a pair of very long and sometimes serrated canine teeth, specially wide-opening jaws and fierce claws to match. The cats as we know them today developed rather later, apparently (if the interpretation is correct) from the sabre-tooths, thus presenting the situation, unusual in palaeontology, where a skeletal feature, having developed itself, has apparently undeveloped itself to maintain the competitiveness of the group—the usual solution is to replace the superseded specialized types with new types from the primitive stock. Alternative interpretations of cat history are available, however.

RODENTIA

This is the most successful and diversified of all mammalian orders. The rodents are characterized by two very long incisors at the front end of each jaw which, unlike human teeth, grow throughout the animal's life to counteract the wear due to the rodents' gnawing propensities. Indeed, to lose a tooth, in depriving the opposite tooth of anything to grind against, may cause the death of the rodent when the tooth grows in a curve till it penetrates the skull. *Eumegamys* of South America was the largest fossil rodent, the skull alone being 2 ft long, and to this day the largest living rodent, the capybara, is a native of South America (4 ft long). Rats and mice date back to the Oligocene, and have gained in importance not only because of their numbers but also for their tenacity of life which enables them to survive in the most adverse circumstances. Thus they are the only placentals other than the dingo (wild dog)—which was probably introduced by man—to have survived the deep waters, presumably on natural rafts of tangled driftwood, from Indonesia to Australia.

OTHER MAMMALIAN ODRERS

The hares and rabbits (Lagomorpha), which are superficially rodent-like, have a long history. The Aardvark, with its cringing appearance, belongs to an order of its own, with a small fossil record. *Arsinoetherium*, the gigantic double-horned beast from the Egyptian Oligocene, defies classification altogether, beyond the fact that it is a mammal, and has been given an order of its own with no known relatives.

GEOGRAPHICAL CONSIDERATIONS IN THE TERTIARY ERA

The emergence of Panama has already been mentioned (see pp. 58–59); also the creation of mountain ranges (see pp. 112–113). It remains to describe the nature and significance of land-bridges (that is, isthmuses), and their function in the Tertiary Era.

There can be no doubt of the existence of land-bridges. A glance at a map of the world will reveal obvious examples at Panama and Suez. Closer inspection will reveal the likely existence of an isthmus, in the recent past, between Alaska and Siberia, since the Bering Sea is very shallow. Less obvious examples exist between Australia and Indonesia; water depths are here much greater than in the Bering Sea, but presumably they could have been rather different in the past in view of the unstable nature of the crust hereabouts, at Gibraltar, and so on. Much of the indirect evidence for past land-bridges comes from comparisons of living fauna across stretches of open sea. Unfortunately it is tempting to postulate wildly on slender evidence, and so many more or less fantastic land-bridges have been suggested in the past that they have become a kind of panacea for otherwise inexplicable biological distributions. Confirmation of suggested land-bridges may be provided by fossils if they are present, but a few cautionary remarks are in order before going on to a discussion of the rôle of land-bridges in palaeontology.

The distribution of certain animals, for instance the tapirs, in extreme parts of the world (in this case South-East Asia and Southern and Central America) may at first glance suggest a trans-Pacific land-bridge in the past (see Fig. 34), but a much more credible explanation is provided by the occurrence of fossil tapirs in Europe, China and North America, thus indicating that tapirs originally roamed the world as a whole, and have in later times been restricted to certain corners of it. The same explanation is valid for the occurrence of marsupials in Australia and South America.

A secondary cautionary consideration is the theory of continental drift. Most continental drift phenomena were complete, or approaching completion, by the later part of the Cenozoic Era, but earlier histories must take drift into account. Thus the occurrence of the trilobite *Olenellus* in the Cambrian rocks of Scotland and Newfoundland suggests that North America was once joined on to Eurasia, and that the Atlantic, as a deep ocean, has opened up since the Cambrian Period. Palaeontological evidence for continental drift is, however, suggestive rather than convincing. Shallow-water marine animals are adept at finding their way across deep oceans via shallow regions, and so on. Fortunately for the drift-minded palaeontologists, however, their theories have been strongly supported by the geophysicists, especially in recent years. Australia seems, on geophysical evidence, to be drifting northward-eastwards, and India to be drifting, or to have drifted, northwards. Carboniferous ice-scratches on boulders in India coming from the direction of the present-day equator suggest that India once lay south of the equator, and in fact it is a central concept of continental drift that South Africa, India, Australia, Antarctica and South America were once a single southern super-continent.

AUSTRALIA

The isolation of Australia throughout the Cenozoic, and that of South America in most of the Tertiary Era, are manifest in the mammal fossil record of these continents. North America and Africa, on the other hand, have never been separated from Eurasia for long, and so effectively belong to the same biogeographical unit. Antarctica formed a further isolated unit in Cenozoic time, and the severity of its glaciation in the later Cenozoic served to add to Antarctica's isolation by adding an ecological barrier to the geographical one.

Australia has a rich marsupial (pouched) fauna — kangaroo,

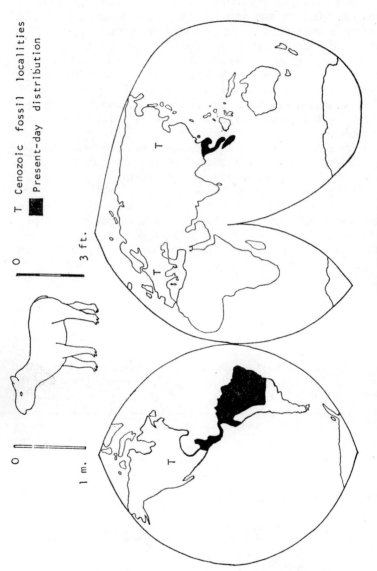

T Cenozoic fossil localities

■ Present-day distribution

Fig. 34 *The distribution of Tapirs*

wombat, koala and so on—which bears evidence of being the relics of a Mesozoic or very early Tertiary fauna. Unfortunately there are not enough vertebrate fossils in Australia to provide us with a history of the diversification of the marsupials. However, it is evident from the modern Australian fauna that:

(1) apart from bats and rodents and the animals that man has introduced, Australia has virtually no placental mammals.
(2) the marsupials, which may have arrived when Australia was joined to the rest of the world in the Mesozoic Era, have diversified into types resembling placental types—pouched 'wolf', 'mouse', and 'anteaters' are all known.
(3) egg-laying mammals (platypus and echidna), probably relics of a fauna older than the marsupials, persist in Australasia.

It should also be noted that the above remarks also apply to New Guinea and other islands of East Indonesia. Furthermore, though no egg-laying mammals occur outside this area, a few marsupials are known (see below), and, in fact, marsupials were common throughout the world in Paleocene times, before being ousted by the placentals. Australasia must, therefore, have once been joined to the rest of the world by a land-bridge.

SOUTH AMERICA

South America, being isolated in Eocene times, held an evolving mixture of marsupial and placental mammals in isolation, until the Central American isthmus re-emerged in the Pliocene. The opossum, which occurs in North and South America today, is one of the few non-Australian marsupial survivors. It is curious how the last South American carnivorous marsupial paralleled the sabre-tooth tiger with its fang-like teeth, while in the Old World and North America the placental sabre-tooths were also thriving, whereas now both types are extinct, presumably reflecting the disappearance of their large, thick-skinned prey. It is generally accepted that the re-emergence of Panama caused widespread depletion of the South American fauna, and indeed there is fossil evidence of the arrival of northern placentals there in the Quaternary era, and concomitant extinctions in the native fauna. But it is curious how the northern species themselves suffered extinctions also, so that South America is today rather thinly populated by mammals compared with, say, Africa. The invasion across the Central American isthmus was not entirely one-sided, and the armadillo, porcupine and ground sloth, to a limited extent, successfully invaded North America.

ANTARCTICA

Antarctica, though providing a 'land-bridge' between the southern continents when they were closer together in the Palaeozoic Era, seems to have been too isolated since then, to receive land-mammals.

FILTER ROUTES

It has been observed in the South Pacific that the further east an island is from Australia the fewer land-mammals and birds there are on it, though the latitude and climate is approximately the same. This is a natural consequence of the well-known filter principle, whereby a barrier exists which some animals can cross and others cannot. The Sahara is a filter, because only certain animals can cross it, and likewise dense jungles and oceans, and indeed any widespread uniform environment may act as a filter and 'sieve out' certain creatures. Some mammals can survive these filters better than others, the rodents being a noticeable example of the former.

OTHER LAND-BRIDGES

The Bering Straits have been emergent several times in the Cenozoic Era, and across their dried-up floor a good many mammals have passed—elephants, musk-ox, sheep, bison, and so on. Sinai and Gibraltar offer further examples of land-bridges, but Africa seems to have been less influenced by isolation than South America or Australia.

NON-MAMMALIAN VERTEBRATES

Compared with the mammals, the rest of the vertebrate phylum seems to have been markedly conservative in the Cenozoic Era. The birds, it is true, exhibit diversification in Cenozoic times, but they are a structurally simple group, with little skeletal variety compared with the mammals, and indeed are still very like reptiles, apart from their warm blood and feathers. Furthermore, bird skeletons are relatively frail and provide few fossils.

Among the reptiles, the turtles and lizards became more developed as the Cenozoic Era proceeded, and crocodile remains are somewhat common in non-marine rocks of the Cenozoic. Snakes occur also in the Cenozoic; a 60 ft specimen is known from the Eocene Period. Poisonous snakes do not seem to have begun till the Miocene Period, however. Amphibian remains are occasionally encountered, but the fish, a still-expanding group, are quite numerous in the fossil record. Frequent fish fossils in the Cenozoic are the scales and vertebrae and the beautifully-preserved sharks' teeth which brighten up many an amateur fossil collection. *Carcharodon megalodus* (Miocene) possessed teeth 5 in long, and may have been about 40 ft long; an impressive length for a carnivorous fish.

THE SARMATIC AREA

A remarkable example of the evidence of fossils in reconstructing the geography of past ages is given by the late Tertiary and Quaternary history of the Sarmatic area (Hungary–Black Sea–Caspian–Aral Sea). As Fig. 35 shows, in the Miocene Period most of this area was a lagoonal basin, apart from the recently-emergent mountains of the Alps, Carpathians, and the Caucasus. That is to say, the area was a brackish lake (i.e. with a salinity less than the open sea but more than fresh water) with the present-day mountains as islands or peninsulas. The evidence for this is provided by the fossils— wherever lagoonal waters exist on any appreciable scale, a characteristic fauna appears therein, and since the Sarmatic area was one of the largest and most persistent brackish lakes of the world, its creatures had a good chance to evolve peculiar types not seen elsewhere in the world.

The intermittent openings of this Miocene brackish lake to the Mediterranean Sea seem to have been north of the Alps, and via the Bosphorus area. It would appear that marine influences penetrated the north-Alpine entrance to this lake in mid-Miocene times, but in the late Miocene the Sarmatic fauna, characterized by brackish water molluscs and occasional mammal beds (the latter being commoner in terrestrial deposits) is in evidence as far west as the Vienna area. In the late Miocene Period, as part of the general tendency towards the uplift and emergence of this part of the Tethys, the lake areas of Sarmatic Europe became more restricted and more distinctive in their fauna.

Mollusca are very common in the Sarmatic rocks, showing the wealth of specimens but poverty in numbers of species that is commonly found in brackish environments where food abounds but the 'wrong' salinity prevents most marine or fresh-water species from living there. The Pannonian Basin (Hungary) became cut off and lost its salinity as it slowly became a fresh-water lake; the

E

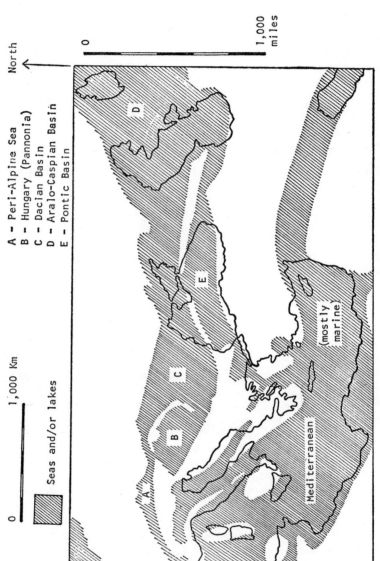

North ←

0   1,000 Km

⬛ Seas and/or lakes

A − Peri-Alpine Sea
B − Hungary (Pannonia)
C − Dacian Basin
D − Aralo-Caspian Basin
E − Pontic Basin

0   1,000 miles

Mediterranean
(mostly marine)

Fig. 35   The Sarmatic area in the Upper Tertiary

eastern Sarmatic area, however, became very rich in its brackish fauna. By the Pliocene Period, the eastern part, also cut off from the sea, began to 'freshen up', and to develop a fauna where, those brackish species which were not replaced by fresh-water types, adapted themselves more and more to the newer, fresher conditions. During the Pliocene Period one finds in the Pannonian (Hungary) area purely fresh-water lake sediments; in the Dacian (Rumania) area a similar situation developing; in the Pontic (Black Sea) area a brackish lake like the modern Caspian; in the Aegean area another lake; and in the Caspian area a brackish region with certain peculiarities.

Since the Tertiary Era, the Pannonian area has virtually dried up, leaving only Lake Balaton to continue the fresh-water tradition, though the original extent of this area can be seen by a glance at any orographic map. The plains of Hungary mark out the old Pannonian lake area, while the ring of mountains around it mark the old shore-line. The Danube penetrates these mountains at the Iron Gate and enters the Dacian basin, another dried-up area, and finally flows into the Black Sea where the brackish conditions have revived as a result of the Quaternary invasion of the sea through the Bosphorus area. However, the new Black Sea fauna is mainly derived from the Mediterranean, and the old Sarmatic fauna was largely destroyed by the invasion of this water, even more saline than the average ocean.

At the present time, the fish of the Black Sea are restricted to the top layers, since the deeper parts (down to 7,000 ft) are choked with the poisonous products of sulphate-reducing bacteria. The Caspian Sea is the one great survivor from the Sarmatic past; at the moment it is a region of greatly contrasting conditions—the northern part freezes in winter, while certain land-locked bays further south become so hot in summer that they evaporate and lay down salt deposits. Similar conditions also occur in the Aral Sea. The Caspian, though its surface has sunk to 92 ft below sea level since its maximum development, is still the largest remnant of the Sarmatic lake, and its fauna is a truly Sarmatic fauna, albeit somewhat reduced from its former state.

The Aegean lake has become largely drowned by the Mediterranean, and its deposits and lake-dwelling fossils have been so riven by earth-movements that they range from 5,000 ft above present-day sea level to well below that level, thus indicating that this area has been broken-up by earth-movements. Greece is, of course, still in a seismically active area. It would be very satisfactory if one could conclude these remarks on the Sarmatic area by giving reasons for this basin-and-barrier formation, but unfortunately the explanation of subcrustal mechanisms is very much a matter of opinion, and, being remote from the subject of palaeontology, it is preferable merely to state here the fossil evidence for the changing salinities.

8   The Quaternary Era

'Out of whose womb came the ice?' – Job 38:29

The Quaternary Era differs from the Tertiary Era mainly in that its climate shows the periodic development of immense ice-sheets in certain parts of the world. The life is but an extension of Tertiary life, but acquires an additional interest from (a) the large size of many of the mammals (b) the existence of species now extinct but contemporaries of early man (c) man himself (d) the reaction of life to the sudden and profound fluctuations of climate in the Quaternary Era.

To deal with the last matter first, we may consider the classic case of the molluscan fauna of the Baltic (see Fig. 36), and its reaction to the events of the recession of the last ice phase. When the last ice phase was at its most rigorous, all North-West Europe was buried under a continental ice-sheet. However, in more recent years the ice has waned with the temporary warming-up of the climate which we are experiencing today, and the following remarks concern later stages of this recession of the ice.

(1) In the Arctic (glacial lake) phases, ice covered most of Scandinavia, and the Baltic was an ice-dammed lake which, when filled with meltwater from the receding ice, finally overflowed through central Sweden to the North Sea. Walrus and polar bear fossils are known from South-West Sweden. These species now live in Spitzbergen, Greenland, and Arctic U.S.S.R.

(2) In the Yoldia phase, approximately 8,000 B.C., shellbanks were laid down in South-West Sweden with molluscs therein of brackish-water types, characteristic of colder water than today's, though not as cold as the Arctic phase. The Yoldia sea occupied the Baltic area, was characterized by the bivalve *Yoldia*, and connected with the Atlantic across Sweden.

(3) In the Ancylus phase, the Baltic became fresh-water again (*Ancylus* is a fresh-water limpet). This was evidently due to the

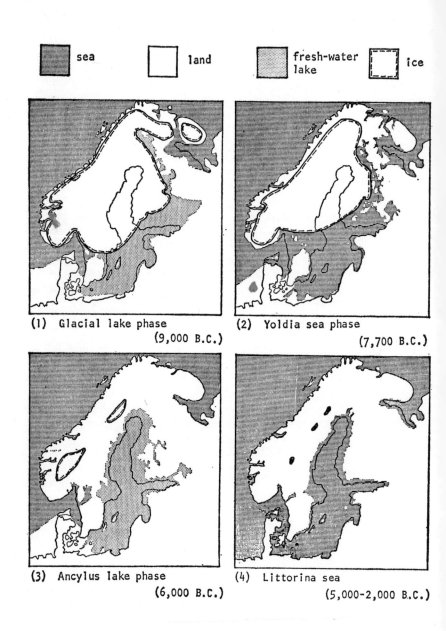

| sea | land | fresh-water lake | ice |

(1) Glacial lake phase
(9,000 B.C.)

(2) Yoldia sea phase
(7,700 B.C.)

(3) Ancylus lake phase
(6,000 B.C.)

(4) Littorina sea
(5,000-2,000 B.C.)

Fig. 36   *The recent history of the Baltic*

rise of Scandinavia as a result of the release of the ice's pressure
on the earth's crust as the ice melted. The crust rises slower than
the ice melts, and so its rise is delayed; in fact Scandinavia is still
rising to this day, and parts of Finland are being uplifted at 1 cm
per year. The south-west coast of Sweden bears Atlantic fossils,
indicating a temperature similar to today's.

(4) The Littorina sea occupied the Baltic (*Littorina* is the winkle,
a marine gastropod). This evidently arose owing to the fact that
the world's sea level was rising (because of the melting ice) faster
than Scandinavia was rising as a release from ice-pressure. The high
sea level may have been aided by the current 'climatic optimum'
of 5,000–2,000 B.C., when the world's temperature was a little
warmer than today's (a difference of the order of 2° C), and the
sea level a little higher. *Littorina* appears as a fossil further inside
the Baltic than it does today, indicating that the Littorina sea was
more saline than the modern Baltic. Furthermore, species surviving
today in the Baltic were larger than now, perhaps reflecting more
marine conditions. Today Baltic shells are often smaller than
Atlantic shells due in part to the brackish nature of the Baltic sea.
Species of mollusc, familiar today along the shores of Britain and
Scandinavia, thrived as far north as Spitzbergen, during the Climatic
Optimum.

(5) Today, after certain other salinity variations, the Baltic is
less saline than in the Littorina phase, being more or less marine
near Denmark, but virtually fresh-water in the inner bays. In the
north it freezes in winter.

The changes of climate during the Quaternary Era are manifest
in many ways, of which the history of the Baltic is but one. Often
the evidence comes from the molluscs, but the evidence tends to
be somewhat indirect. Mammals may also be used for the same
purpose, and in fact nearly all fossils can be considered for their
evidence of the Quaternary environment. The general conclusion
to be reached from the evidence (both fossil and non-fossil), is that
ice periodically appeared in large areas of the world (see Fig. 37),
and that it is now in a phase of recession, though of course extensive ice-sheets still exist in Antarctica, Greenland and elsewhere.
There is no definite evidence that the ice will or will not return
to its former extent. It may come as a surprise to the novice that
most of Canada was once glaciated, that pack-ice once filled the
North Atlantic between Britain and North America, that the Rhône
glacier of the Alps was once over 100 miles long (it is now 8 miles
long) and reached as far as Lyons, and that the mountains of
Australia and Tasmania were once glacier-bearing.

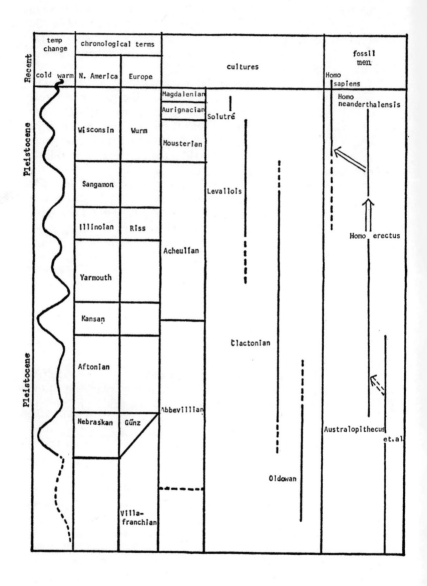

Fig. 37   Quaternary events and man's history

Fossils, of course, seldom give evidence of actual ice, but they do give evidence of a fluctuating environment, in the manner explained below, and the presence of large ice-sheets in the world can be inferred from the evidence from the fossils of changing temperatures:

(1) Direct evidence of cold water, derived from the study of oxygen isotope ratios in fossil remains (see pp. 31–32).

(2) Distribution of non-extinct species and varieties, compared with their present environment.

(3) Distribution of non-extinct genera (occasionally larger groups) allowing for the environmental latitude of the genera considered (see p. 112).

(4) Stunting and other physiological changes brought about by a changing environment.

Many difficulties stand in the way of the interpretation of fossil evidence of changing temperatures. Among them are:

(a) Fossils may be derived—that is, washed into rocks of a different age to that of the fossil itself.

(b) Fossils are seldom found exactly where the organism died. Wood drifts, shells are wafted over the sea floor by currents, dead land vertebrates float out to sea and rot and shed their bones in the 'wrong' environment.

(c) Species can sometimes, though probably rarely, change their environment (see p. 37). A change of environment usually causes a change of species by evolution.

Furthermore, evidence for cold temperatures may not in itself be evidence of extensive glaciation of the earth:

(i) glaciation is due to cold and precipitation, not cold alone. Siberia is colder than Iceland, but is less glaciated owing to the former's dryness.

(ii) cold water may arise from a fall in water-level causing barriers to emerge which cut off warm currents, or from a rise in water-level causing straits to open which let in cold currents.

(iii) cold water is denser than warm water, and hence it sinks; so temperatures may fall if the water deepens even though the climate of the world is constant.

It may seem from all this that it is amazing how fossils can be used to indicate temperatures at all! However, by patient work and wide-ranging knowledge, the palaeontologist can draw the skein of evidence together. Since so many errors can arise, it is seldom that the evidence of a single fossil species can be utilized; if a large number of species can be found, then certain statements about the environment can be cautiously made. When in conjunction with non-fossil evidence, such as ice-scratchings and salt deposits, the periodic glaciation of the earth's surface in the Quaternary emerges as an incontrovertible fact. Local variations on this theme complicate matters, but the general trend of events is clear enough. Thus there were four major glaciations in the Alps, but in Britain only three. Antarctica, though undergoing an interglacial phase now, is still glaciated, so owing to the quantity of its ice it 'misses' interglacials, and may give evidence of deceptively few glacial phases in the Quaternary Era.

Indeed, the above-mentioned principles can be applied to the Cenozoic Era as a whole, and it is intriguing to see how the temperature of the world falls after the Eocene Period, as if in preparation for the coming glaciations. It is not the place of a book on palaeontology to discuss the causes of glaciations or their periodicity, but it can briefly be said that there is an abundance of hypotheses on this subject, and that these hypotheses range from the cooling of the sun itself, to the redistribution of the continents by continental drift and consequent restriction of the influence of the ocean currents. Fossils, needless to say, are as mute in their evidence of the mechanisms at work as they are eloquent in their evidence of the consequences of glaciation.

THE MAMMALIA

In terms of evolution, the Quaternary mammals are but an extension of the Tertiary mammals already described, but additional notes may be made on those which have gained importance in the literature through their large size, or their associations with man. The large size of the Quaternary mammals is a difficult matter to decide, since it is not easy to say exactly what one means by 'large size'. Many Pleistocene mammals were larger than their Tertiary or Recent relatives, but it is an indistinct tendency. The *average* size of the mammals may have declined in the Pleistocene with respect to the Tertiary owing to the ascendancy of the rodents; the largest land mammal of all (*Baluchitherium*) was of Tertiary age. Yet it is very striking how so many mammals today have large Pleistocene relatives. The cause of this is obscure. The cold of the Pleistocene could be quoted, but small mammals like the lemmings can survive in cold climates, and in any case, intense cold is a temporary and fluctuating characteristic of the Quaternary Era. At any rate, the following examples of Pleistocene gigantism can be drawn up.

Marsupialia: *Diprotodon* was like the living wombat in appearance, but was the size of a rhinoceros. It was so large that its bones were at first thought to be those of an elephant.

Primates: gigantic 'ape-men' have been reported from the Pleistocene of Java, but not enough material is available to be certain that the remains are anything other than those of a particularly large individual of the *Homo [Pithecanthropus] erectus*.

Artiodactyla (cloven-hoofs): the 'Irish Elk' (Fig. 38) was a giant deer with the largest recorded antlers (up to 11 ft span). That early man knew it personally is evident from the painting of it at Cougnac, France (probably c. 15,000 B.C.). It ranged from Ireland to Siberia. In North America a giant moose arose. The modern American moose and European elk are of the same species—*Alces alces*, whereas the 'Irish Elk' is *Megaceros*, and not an elk at all. Pleistocene bison in North America had horns up to 10 ft span.

Edentata (mammals with reduced teeth, mostly in South America): *Glyptodon*, a sort of giant armadillo, grew up to 9 ft long and must have been one of the largest armoured animals since the Mesozoic: a related genus had a weighted, mace-like tail curiously similar to that of the Mesozoic ankylosaurs (see p. 101). *Megatherium*, the giant ground-sloth, grew up to 18 ft long, an almost dinosaurian size. Another giant sloth, *Grypotherium*, was found in a Patagonian cave in conditions which suggested that it had been kept in captivity by man and killed for food, a few centuries ago.

Proboscidea: *Mastodon* was not particularly large by elephantine standards. The woolly mammoth (*Mammuthus primigenius*) was no bigger than the modern elephants, but with its shaggy, yak-like coat, huge head and enormous recurved horns may have looked bigger (see Fig. 39). *Palaeoloxodon antiquus*, however, was an elephant 13 ft high at the shoulders (large African bull elephants reach 11 ft); a specimen in England was 12 ft 7 ins high and still not adult.

Carnivora: the bears developed a large Pleistocene type in the form of *Ursus spelaeus*, the cave bear, though it was only fractionally larger than certain modern bears. The sabre-toothed tiger, though famous for its great teeth, was no larger than the modern tiger or lion, and in fact its powerful feet and short legs suggest that it preferred to ambush its prey rather than to stalk and charge like the present-day cats. A giant cheetah, *Acinonyx jubatus*, occurs in the Old World Lower Pleistocene. This form later developed into the modern cheetah which, though smaller in size, is still sufficiently well-built to hold the record for being the fastest-running land animal today.

Fig. 38   *The 'Irish Elk' (Megaceros)*

Fig. 39   *The Mammoth (Mammuthus)*

Rodentia : the rodents were never very large creatures, but *Eumegamys*, of the South American Pleistocene, may have reached the size of an ox, or at any rate a good deal larger than the largest living rodent, the capybara, which is approximately 3–4 ft long.

It should be noted that many groups have been omitted from this list, e.g. horses and whales, since their largest forms are still extant today in the Recent epoch, and other orders have their giant forms in the Tertiary Era. The cats, on the other hand, developed along sabre-tooth lines to a large size, only to be replaced today by the true cats, which are not closely related to the sabre-tooth, but have a very similar size.

What is so very much more striking than the mere size of the large Pleistocene mammals, is the fact that so many of them are now extinct, often for no very obvious reason. The predatory activities of man may have been a factor, but not the only one. Both the camel and the horse are essentially creatures of North American origin; they spread to the Old World via the dried-up Bering Straits in the Pleistocene Period, and thrived in the Old World (where man was old-established) but died out in the Americas (where man arrived late). On being re-introduced to the Americas, both camels and horses flourished once more in their particular environments. It may be noted in this connection that early man hunted horses for food, as indicated by thousands of horse skeletons at the foot of 1,000 ft cliff—over which they were presumably driven by man—in France.

There are, of course, many examples of extinctions clearly due to man himself, more especially among the flightless birds. Feathers of the giant ostrich-like moa were found round native camp-fires by the first white settlers in New Zealand, though the white man never actually saw a living moa. The dodo disappeared from its only home in Mauritius in the seventeenth century owing to the arrival of hungry sailors from Europe. The last wolf in Britain was shot in 1743. Some mammals died out in the early Pleistocene Period, when men were too few and too primitive to have much effect of any sort on the world's ecology—many, of course, had died out long before the Quaternary Era and its men had arrived at all. Many factors have been at work—climatic, geographical, predator/prey relationships, and simple competition from similar but better developed types.

Especially interesting from our own point of view is the evidence of the co-existence of early man with animals now extinct or restricted to more remote environments. Thus in Kent's Cavern, in England, there are two entrances to the cave-system; in one, evidence of Palaeolithic man is to be found, while in the other, there are the gnawed and cracked bones typical of a hyaena's lair, along with bones of the hyaenas themselves, and also a wolf's lair. It is seldom easy to establish exact contemporaneity in palaeontology, but it has been claimed that the thick layers of charcoal in a connecting-passage between the humans' quarters and the beasts' quarters are remains of a barrier of fires maintained by man to keep the hyaenas and wolves at bay while he lived in his own part of the cave, perhaps enabling him to prey on them when food was scarce in the winter. It seems a horrifyingly precarious existence, but at any rate it would appear evident that man and hyaena and wolf lived at more or less the same time in this quiet part of England in the Pleistocene Period.

Proof of the co-existence of man and mammals now extinct, comes from the painted caves in France and Spain of the late Pleistocene Period. Here, executed with first-class artistry, are clearly recognizable pictures of mammoth and woolly rhinoceros, clothed with flesh and hair. More commonly seen are species not yet extinct but unfamiliar today in the region where the paintings are now to be found—thus bison, hyaena, and reindeer were all clearly familiar to the cave-painters of France and Spain. Today the bison is very rare in Europe, the hyaena is restricted to Africa and Asia, and reindeer have retreated towards the Arctic.

MAN

Man himself provides us with a disappointing fossil record. His fossils are rare, and his beginnings are indistinct—arguments continually arise over points of nomenclature and dating—but one may broadly say that the history of the genus *Homo* is more or less co-incident with the Quaternary Era, and that of the species *Homo sapiens* is restricted to the later Pleistocene and Recent, though there have recently been suggestions that the genus *Homo* was present in the Upper Pliocene of Kenya. The structural changes from ape to man include the following:

(1) increase in skull capacity: roughly from 500 cc to 1,500 cc (not all at once, however).
(2) development from the 'receding chin' of the ape to the 'square jaw' of modern man.
(3) increasing perfection of the upright stance.
(4) reduction in size of the canine teeth.
(5) a development towards the verticality in the facial profile, promoted by the increased size of the forehead.
(6) decrease in size of the eyebrow-ridges.

These, and other structural modifications reflect the human preference for walking and running to climbing—indicating a departure from forest life—and an increased mental adaptation to the intricacies of social life. The study of fossil man, itself a difficult enough undertaking, is not made any easier by its attraction for practical jokers. The so-called Piltdown Man of Sussex (England), which haunted text-books for 40 years, has now been revealed as the offspring of a fraudulent marriage between an ape's jaw and a human skull, and probably neither of them was as old as the age originally attributed to them. On the other hand, it has been claimed that Neanderthal man gained much of his stooping, bent-forward structure, which so contributes to the bestiality of the appearance of reconstructions of his figure, from the fact that one of the accounts of him was based on a skeleton afflicted by osteoarthritis. In fact, he probably stood upright like us. It has been observed that the skull of Homo [Pithecanthropus] erectus, though markedly smaller than ours, bears evidence of a weakly-developed speech-centre, this suggesting that an incipient ability to make himself intelligible to his comrades, with all that entails in social advancement, had begun. Homo neanderthalensis, like Homo sapiens, had the use of fire, buried his dead, and hunted the woolly rhinoceros, cave bear, and so on.

Events during the Pleistocene Period were not, on the whole, much influenced by man's development, since while he was a hunter and dependent on the game on which he preyed he could not multiply greatly because of the constant threat of starvation. The situation must have been analogous to North America or Africa before the arrival of the white man: scattered tribes of hunters, practising animistic religions, and kept few in number by the high infant mortality and high death-rate — most Neanderthal skeletons belonging to individuals over 30 years of age are male, suggesting that death by childbirth was the common fate of the female—living in a land often teeming with game. Examples of the abundance of large mammals in the Pleistocene Period come from many fossil-finds rich in mammals but with little or no human remains. In the tar-pit of Los Angeles, not only are numerous elephantids and other herbivores to be found, but also the sabre-tooth 'tigers' that preyed on them, and vultures that scavenged the remains. (Teratornis, a vulture from the Los Angeles Pleistocene, is the largest flying bird on record.)

QUATERNARY LAND-BRIDGES AND ISLANDS

Mammals were probably most numerous and various in Africa and Eurasia. Large numbers penetrated into North America in the Pleistocene Period with the periodic emergence of the Bering Straits, and some proceeded to South America across Panama. Australia, however, and many islands, received negligible mammal invasions during the Pleistocene, with resultant developments of strange indigenous faunas. The fate of the animals trapped on islands differs greatly due to a variety of factors. In Malta, for example, formerly joined by a land-bridge to Sicily and hence to Europe, caves contain the fossils of dwarf elephants and dwarf hippopotami.

The explanation has been given that these animals, formerly of large size, had become stunted owing to lack of food when Malta became an island. On other islands, however, animals have grown and thrived to an exceptionally large size; for example, the Quaternary elephant-birds of Madagascar and moas of New Zealand, both about 14 ft tall, died out only a few centuries ago, and there are the giant tortoises—still surviving—on the Galapagos islands.

THE RECENT EPOCH

With the last retreat of the ice, the Pleistocene Period merges into the Recent Epoch. By common consent the latter begins at c. 9,000 B.C. Thus we come to the historical time, when man, released from the population restrictions inherent in a hunting mode of life, began to take up farming and thus to multiply on the face of the earth and bring it into the state of civilization which we now know. The Recent is the phase where palaeontology fades discreetly into the background, and archaeology takes over, and is thus the end of the subject of this book. It is, perhaps, appropriate at this point to mention the full turn of the circle in referring to man's history as a fossil collector.

The earliest known examples of fossils as objects of man's curiosity come from some of the earliest known remains of *Homo sapiens*; thus Crô-Magnon man (10,000–30,000 years ago) collected crystals and ammonite shells. The Plains Indians of North America have kept fossils in special bags as 'medicine'. Sometimes the shells were cut up and strung like beads as 'wampum'. Bones of the giant Oligocene mammal, *Brontotherium*, were found by Red Indians and called 'thunder-horses', supposing them to come from animals which descended to earth in thunderstorms. Modern palaeontology has take the name *Brontotherium* directly from this legend (Greek bronte: thunder, ther: animal). Siberian natives have long known the fossil horns of the now extinct woolly rhinoceros, calling them 'griffins' in allusion to their supposed association with large mythical birds.

Early man presumably did not know what the fossils were, but merely collected them because of their intrinsic attractiveness. Though the Greeks and Romans were aware of the existence of fossils in the Mediterranean area, and sometimes correctly identified them for what they were, they did not properly realize how the fossils came to be there. It was not until da Vinci, who not only understood that the fossils which he saw in the hills of northern Italy were of marine Mollusca, but also realized that they must have arrived when the Mediterranean formerly covered what is now dry land, that the science of true palaeontology began to emerge. Da Vinci also saw that the fossils of the East of Europe indicated the former existence of a great sea, of which the Caspian, Black Sea and Hungarian lakes are shrivelled-up remnants. We now know that he was correct in this deduction, for he was looking at the Sarmatic area (see pp. 129–132). He even suggested that the Mediterranean and Red seas were once connected via Sinai, a premonition of Tethys.

Da Vinci was, of course, ahead of his time in scientific thought, but eventually the rest of the human race caught up with his ideas, and the theory that fossils were minerals which grew in situ in the rock was finally replaced by the concept of fossils as enunciated in this book.

List of Illustrations

Glossary of Technical Terms

AGNATHA   A group of jawless fish, (e.g. the lamprey).

ALGAE   A group of plants which includes the modern seaweeds.

AMMONITE   An extinct type of cephalopod mollusc in which the suture is particularly complex.

AMMONOID   An extinct type of cephalopod mollusc in which the suture is folded. The ammonoids are subdivided, according to the complexity of the suture, into goniatites, ceratites and ammonites.

ARCHOSAURIA   Reptiles, mostly extinct, commonly of a large size, including the so-called 'dinosaurs', crocodiles, pterodactyls, etc.

ARTHROPODA   A large group of animals usually having a jointed external skeleton of chitinous material (e.g. insects, crabs, lobsters, spiders, trilobites).

BELEMNITE   A term variously used for the bullet-shaped calcareous fossils which were the internal skeletons of certain extinct cephalopods, or for the animals which owned them.

BELEMNOID   An extinct type of cephalopod, the internal shells of which are commonly termed belemnites.

BENTHOS, BENTHIC   Benthos is the life living on the sea-floor; benthic is an adjectival form of the word.

BIVALVE   A member of the phylum Mollusca, the shell being in two halves (valves), (e.g. cockle, mussel, oyster).

BRACHIOPODA   A group of marine, bivalved animals looking superficially like the true bivalves, but having one valve generally larger than the other, each valve being itself bilaterally symmetrical.

BRYOZOA   A group of tiny colonial aquatic animals; the appearance of their colonies in life has given rise to their nickname 'moss animals'. They often build calcareous structures which fossilise.

CALCAREOUS   Containing calcium carbonate.

CALCICHORDATA   An extinct group of fossils whose properties indicate affinity both with the echinoderms and with, or inclusion in, the chordates.

CEPHALOPOD   A type of marine mollusc with the head surrounded by tentacles. Fossils include ammonoids, nautiloids and belemnites.

CHITIN, CHITINOUS   Chitin is a horn-like substance of the carbohydrate type used in the skeletons of certain animals, (e.g. arthropods). Chitinous is the adjectival form.

CHORDATA   The group of animals which includes the verte- brates (i.e. those with a spinal column, e.g. fish, reptiles, mammals).

CLASS   A biological division of life, being a subdivision of a phylum, (e.g. the Class Mammalia (mammals)).

COELENTERATA   A group of animals including the jellyfish and corals, characterized by simple soft parts and radial symmetry in their construction.

CRINOID   A type of echinoderm having a superficial plant-like appearance—a stem, a rotund body and arms which are located on the top of the animal .

CROSSOPTERYGIAN   A type of fish characterized by a fleshy lobe at the base of the fin.

ECHINODERM   A member of the marine phylum Echinoder- mata, which is characterized by five-fold symmetry and a complex skeleton of calcium carbonate plates.

ECHINOID   A type of echinoderm having a rotund body, the outside of which is protected by an armoury of spines.

FORAMINIFERA   One-celled creatures whose tiny skeletons (usually calcium carbonate) form commonly-occurring micro- fossils.

GASTROPOD   A type of mollusc which usually bears a screw- shaped shell (e.g. snails, whelks, etc.).

GENUS   A biological division of life, being a subdivision of an order and generally including several species which are closely related by evolution.

GRAPTOLITE   An extinct colonial organism with a chitinous skeleton which is toothed like a saw.

HOMOEOMORPHOUS   A property of organisms, or their fossils, which exhibits marked similarity and form although the ancestry of each is known to be different from the others' (e.g. whale and ichthyosaur).

HOMOLOGOUS   A property of organisms, or their fossils, which by the similarity of certain features indicates a common ancestry (e.g. man's hand, seal's flipper and bat's wing).

IRON PYRITES   A hard, brassy-yellow mineral. Iron sulphide (FeS_2).

MARSUPIALS   Primitive mammals whose young are borne in a pouch on the female's body (e.g. kangaroo).

MOLLUSC   A large group of animals, living and fossil, commonly characterized by their soft bodies and hard calcium carbonate shells (e.g. bivalves, gastropods and cephalopods).

MONOTREMES   Primitive mammals which reproduce by the laying of eggs (e.g. platypus).

NEKTON   Life which swims in water, usually consisting of large animals (e.g. fish and squids).

ORDER   A biological division of life, being a subdivision of a class, (e.g. the Order Primates (monkeys, apes and man)).

OSTRACODS   Tiny bivalved crustaceans whose shells look superficially like those of true bivalves, but are much smaller than the latter, being barely visible to the naked eye.

PHYLUM   A major biological division. Chordates (vertebrates etc.), molluscs and arthropods form the phyla Chordata, Mollusca and Arthropoda respectively.

PLACENTALS   Mammals with no pouch for bearing the young and having a well-developed placenta. Most mammals alive today are of this type, (e.g. whales, bats, dogs, bears, man).

PLACODERMS   A group of extinct primitive fish which possess jaws.

PLANKTON   Life which drifts in water usually consisting of tiny plants and animals.

PYRITES   Same as Iron Pyrites, q.v.

SPECIES   No exact single definition is possible: in the biology of living organisms a species normally exhibits fertile interbreeding within the group: in palaeontology the interbreeding criterion is beyond proof, so the term is used to group together fossils which are sufficiently similar to each other to be given the same name.

TRILOBITE   An extinct marine member of the phylum Arthropoda, characterized by a three-fold division of the skeleton into cephalon (head) thorax (body) and pygidium (tail), and also a three-fold division longitudinally into lateral and central parts.

ZONE   A small division of rock usually considered to be characterized by its peculiar fossil or fossils, which do not occur above or below the zone; or, the time-interval during which such a rock was formed.

Suggested Further Reading

Recommendations for further reading depend on the reader's intentions. If he is more interested in the dinosaurs, for instance, the books by Edwin H. Colbert will prove fascinating while requiring little or no scientific background knowledge to appreciate them. Other works on vertebrates include the British Museum publications, which are lucid, authoritative and inexpensive. Palaeoecology is dealt with in a commendably readable and straightforward fashion by D. V. Ager in his *Palaeoecology*. There are many books on fossil man, some of them excellent, while others are decidedly diffuse and unscientific. The reader is directed to the British Museum publication on the Primates as a sound basis for further study.

In the wider field of geology, which is inseparable from palaeontology if one is to gain a balanced view of the history from the Earth, the *Principles of Physical Geology* by Arthur Holmes is an excellent source of the grand view of how the various parts of geology knit together. His chapters on Earth history, coal and oil, and marine sediments have a strong relevance to palaeontology. The book is worth having for its illustrations alone.

EDWIN H. COLBERT
Dinosaurs: their discovery and their world (Hutchinson : London, 1962)
Men and dinosaurs: the search in field and laboratory (Evans : London, 1968)
BRITISH MUSEUM PUBLICATIONS
The succession of life through geological time (K. P. Oakley & H. Muir-Wood)
Fossil Amphibians and Reptiles (W. E. Swinton)
History of the Primates (Wilfred le Gros Clark)
Fossil birds (W. E. Swinton)

D. V. AGER
   Paleoecology (McCraw-Hill: New York, 1963)
ARTHUR HOLMES
   Principles of Physical Geology (Nelson: London, 1969)

Some authors, in addition to those already mentioned, are notable
for the lucid style of their writing.
A. J. Arkell   (Jurassic; ammonites)
W. H. Easton   (invertebrate Palaeontology)
A. S. Romer   (vertebrate Palaeontology)

   When identifying specimens collected in the field, the collector
should use publications relevant to the continent he is working
in, since fossil species vary too much from one part of the world
to the other for general publications to be useful, except for certain wide-ranging species. As a rule, the nearer the place where
the fossils are found is to where the book's fossils were found, the
better the chances are of them being satisfactorily identified. In
Britain, three publications by the British Museum are essential
for the amateur collector:

                    British Cenozoic Fossils
                    British Mesozoic Fossils
                    British Palaeozoic Fossils

Index

aardvark, 124
abyss, 60–61
Acanthodii, 81
Acinonyx jubatus, 139
Actinopterygii, 81
active bivalves, characters of, 34, 36
Aegean area, 131
aerial, 10
aerobic life, beginnings of, 42–46
Agnatha and placoderms, 78–81, (79)
Alaska, coexistence of forests and ice, 33
Alces alces, 139
algae, 10, 42
Alps, fossil evidence for their conditions of formation, 112–113
alteration of original material in fossils, 12
amber and fossil insects, 13
American non-marine life, as affected by Panama isthmus, 59
ammonites, (66) (67), 92, 96–98
    extinction at end of the Cretaceous, 98, 108
    in lithographic limestone, 57
Ammonoidea, 92, (93), 94, 96, 97
Amnigenia, a Devonian non-marine bivalve, 84
amphibians, 83–84
Ampullarius, an amphibian gastropod, 69
anaerobic bacteria, their ability to live in a non-oxygenic environment, 41
Anapsida, in reptile classification, 99
Ancylus, 133
angiosperm flora, 95
anisomyarian bivalves, 34–35
Antarctica, fossil wood, 15–16
    lack of mammals in, 128
Antiarchi, 78, 80–81
Apatosaurus, 102
Archaeopteryx, 29, (30), 57–58
'archetype' conception, 22
archetype, gastropod, 62
Archosauria, 94, 99–104, (103)
Arctic, evidence of former warmth there, 16
Arctic phases (of Baltic Quaternary), 133
Argonauta, egg-case of, 65
Arsinoetherium, 124
Arthrodira, 78, 80–81
Arthropoda, 47, 52, 57, 70–71
Artiodactyla, 116, 118, 139
Astrapotherium, 120
atmosphere, Precambrian, 40–42, 46
attitudes of fossils, 33–36
Australasia, gap in the mammal history, 106
Australia, 124, 125, 127
    the great Barrier Reef, 51
    Precambrian fossils, 42–44

156

INDEX

footprints, fossil, 12, 109
Foraminifera, 71–73, 111–112
fossilization, 11–14
fossil names, 9–10, 15
fossils, climatic evidence from, 137
fossils, nature of, 10–14

Galapagos, giant tortoises, 145
Galeopithecus, 117
gastropods, 69–70, 111
genus, 9–10
geological column, 10, (18–19)
German Jurassic reefs, 56–57
giant pigs, 118
Ginkgo, 95
glaciers, 33, 89, 137
Glossopteris, 87
Glyptodon, 121, 139
Gondwanaland ice, 87, 89
Goniatitina, 92, (93), 96
gorilla, 117
graptolites, 14
grass, 95
Great Barrier Reef, 51
Great Basin (USA), paleoecology, 37–38
Greenland, 95
'griffins', 145
ground-sloths, 121, 139
growth-lines, information derived from them, 75–76
Grypotherium, 139
Gunflint Iron formation fossils, 42
gymnosperms, 86

habitats, 30–31, 36–38
hardrosaurs, 99–100
Helix, 70
herbivore teeth, 38
Herodotus, his observations of Foraminifera, 112
Hesperornis, 106
heteromorphic ammonites, (67)
heteropods, 111
hippopotamus, 118, 144
history of Cambrian life, (48), 46–50

history of life, (45)
Hominoidea, 116–117
homoeomorphy, 20, (22)–23, 94, 97, 119–120
'Homo Diluvii Testis' (a fossil salamander), 14
Homo erectus, evidence of speech centres, 144
Homo, fossil record, 143
homology, 20, (22)
Homo neanderthalensis, 144
hoofed mammals, 118–120
horses, 20, (21), 119, 142
Hungary, 131
hyaenas in Kent's Cavern, 142
hydrogen exploding in our galaxy, 109
hyomandibular bone, 28
Hypsilophodon, 99
Hyracotherium, (21), 119

ice, and glaciation, 89, 133–137
ichthyosaurs, 38, 99, 108
Ictidosauria, 26
Iguanodon, 99
imperfection in the fossil record, 23–24
impregnation, as a mode of fossilization, 12
impressions, as fossils, 12
incus, homology of, (27), 28
India, 125
indirect evidence of fossilization, 12–13
Indopacific mollusca, 111
Indricotherium, 114, (115)
inequilateral bivalve shape, 34, (35)
inequivalve bivalve shape, 34, (35)
Insectivora, 116, 117
insectivore teeth, 38
insects, 13, 57, 107, 111
'Irish Elk' (Megaceros), 139, (140)
iron pyrites, 12, 41
island faunas, 144–145

Jamaica, its gastropod fauna, 70
Jamoytius kerwoodi, 78